Overcoming Rejection Will Make You Rich

D1124274

12 ways to turn rejection into unlimited

abundance, success, and freedom

Larry DiAngi

Overcoming Rejection Will Make You Rich
12 ways to turn rejection into unlimited abundance, success and freedom
ISBN 13 978-0-9762765-2-4
ISBN 10 0-9762765-2-6

www.larrydiangi.com
Larry DiAngi Productions
P. O. Box 9056
Erie, PA 16505
Phone (800) 690-1372
Copyright © 2006 by Larry DiAngi

Printed in the United States of America

*This book is dedicated to my father,
who has always totally believed in me
and my purpose. I am thankful for
your unwavering love and support.
Even during the times when it seemed
like I would never get to the next
higher level of my dream-purpose,
you were always there to give me
encouragement. There have
been many times when
your rock solid belief in me was what
I needed to keep moving forward.
Dad, I love you and I am
grateful to have been blessed with
you as my father and loving friend.*

Table of Contents

Chapter

1

Rise to a Higher Level
Where Rejection Can't Touch You

Don't be average. Average people are mostly negative.

Why is it that some people can encounter a large amount of rejection and still come back again and again to readjust their approach and become stronger than ever, while other people can experience just one dose of rejection, and it will stop them from even thinking about going to their next higher level in life? *Average people don't build anyway Biz*

One reason why many people give up so easily at the first sign of rejection is that they don't understand that every perceived rejection needs to be qualified. A rejection should never be taken at face value. For all we know, the person who seems to be rejecting us could be faking it. That individual may be responding to us in a negative way because he or she is too ashamed to admit to not fully understanding what we are talking about, so to "save face" and not appear ignorant or naïve, a person could simply say, "No, I'm not interested in what you are proposing."

Why does the average person either accept rejection as a personal insult or automatically assume that the one who is doing the rejecting is somehow probably right?

In my experience of continuously working with people and being involved in various negotiations, I discovered

There could be several persons why on Average person Rejects you.

that when I first proposed a new idea, there were times when people appeared to be rejecting me, but actually they were just preoccupied with other thoughts at the moment and could not fully concentrate on what I was saying.

They may have had a disagreement with a friend or their spouse earlier that day, and their mind was still clouded by the lingering affect of that altercation. It's possible they were not going to respond positively to anything that anyone proposed to them that day until they got back on good terms with whomever they'd had the conflict.

The list of reasons is endless of why a person's first reaction to us may be something less than positive, and it is almost always wise to give people a second, or even a third, chance to accept the idea we are proposing to them.

Live FAR ABOVE the enemy called "average"

As you read this book you will have the opportunity to neutralize rejection and eliminate the negative effects of rejection forever. But before this is possible you must completely separate yourself from the enemy called "average"

Theodore Roosevelt spoke these heart-strengthening words "I choose not to be a common man. It's my right to be uncommon if I can. I'll seek opportunity, not security. I do not wish to be a kept citizen, humbled and dulled by having the state look after me. I want to take the calculated risk, to dream and to build, to fail and to succeed. I'll refuse to live from hand to mouth. I prefer the challenges of life to the guaranteed existence, the thrill of fulfillment to the calm stale of Utopia. I will never cower before any master, nor bend to any threat. It is my heritage to stand erect, proud and unafraid, to think and act for myself and face the world boldly and say, This I have done."

I believe that every human being has a great destiny to fulfill. If we follow the crowd, we will probably fulfill only an average destiny at best. To break through to a higher level in life, relationships, or business, we must break free from the thinking that holds us down to the level of average, or even below average, perception. Living an above average life and achieving above average results will require that we be able to see life and achievement with an ABOVE average perception.

If we share a vision, idea, or an opportunity with people who have an average perception of life, they may not "get" what we are talking about at first. In fact, much of the rejection thrown at us from a person who has only an average perception may not have anything to do with us or anything we may have said to them. It requires discernment on our part to read people accurately and to see that some may have personal problems that need to be fixed before they are ready to hear what we have to say.

This does not apply to everyone that we encounter, but in studying the state of human beings, it doesn't take long to discover that the average person is more of a pessimist than an optimist. It takes a deliberate effort and approach for a person to stay optimistic on a daily basis. To be pessimistic, a person only has to follow the rest of the world, and their pessimism will be reinforced by society, the media, advertising, their employer, family members, education, and thousands of other negative influences.

So if you and I are involved in the pursuit of building a vision, a mission, or a business that necessitates meeting and talking with new people every day, we can pretty much figure that the majority of new people we encounter are going to be more prone to see only the limitations of life rather than the great possibilities of life. My intention is not to be mean or unkind by stating that, "The average person's outlook on life is more negative than positive." This is just a reality of the world in which we live.

The good news is that we can help some people change their perceptions and thereby help them to create and enjoy greater freedom and literally help them to revolutionize their lives.

SPECIAL NOTE: From this point on in this book I will use the words he and she interchangeably when referring to a person in the singular. The only reason that I will be doing this is to include both men and women equally when I make reference to a person or individual. None of these references are meant to put more emphasis on the masculine or feminine or vice versa in connection with the specific thought I am writing about. I will use the word "he" fifty percent of the time and "she" fifty percent of the time as well.

Some people's first reaction is a preprogrammed automatic response

The reason why some people will reject you or your ideas is that they have already rejected the positive picture of themselves and have rejected any possibility for a better personal future.

Their self-esteem may have been so badly beaten up in the past, that by the time you or I get to them and say, "Hi, how are you," their first thought is, "Why is this person pretending to care about how I am doing? This person doesn't even know me and much less care about the quality of my life"

If this thought or some other skeptical thought is running through the head of the person with whom you are talking, you could simply accept this individual's first response and write this person off as just another rejection. By putting too much importance on people's first reaction to us, we may possibly misread a person's real need and potential. **If we really want to help people, we need to be**

'thick skinned' enough to not be thrown off track by their first reaction. *Period*

The longer I live and the more successful, purpose-driven people I am privileged to meet and develop relationships with, the more I am convinced that one of the greatest secrets to success in any area of life is the ability to keep moving forward in the face of rejection.

Rejection is an interesting thing. None of us like it, so most people try to avoid it. But if we avoid rejection, we are also simultaneously avoiding success.

Winning in life is more important than winning a popularity contest

To rise to a higher level where rejection can't touch us we must also break free from the belief that we need to get everyone to like us. It has become accepted as "common thinking" that one of the main objectives in life is to win a "lifelong popularity contest," and if we can just get everyone to like us, somehow this will make us a better person. Like dropping a coin into a wishing well, some people live with the misguided belief that other people hold the key to their success. If they could just get the right people to like or love them, one of those people would give them a "lucky break" and give them the ability to make their dreams come true.

It is not uncommon for people to believe that the only way they could become highly successful in life is if someone else made it happen for them. Many people do not believe they can create their own success but instead have a fantasy similar to the scenario of a big movie director from Hollywood seeing them in the grocery store and yelling down the aisle of the frozen food section to them, "You're the one. You're the one!!! I've been looking for you! I'm going to make you a star. I'm going to make you rich and famous beyond your wildest dreams!!!"

We have heard people say this phrase over and over: "It's not what you know, but who you know that really matters most." The truth is, it is just the opposite! What you know about yourself and what you know about other people are far more important than simply gaining access to the individuals who are considered to be Big Shots or VIPs. More important than "who you know" is "who will really want to know you!" One way to avoid being negatively affected by rejection is to make sure that we do not allow ourselves to become too dependant on needing the approval of others. The only people who are nourishing for us to know are those who have a high level of integrity and a sincere desire to appreciate us for who we really are. People are important, but for the most part, people are most interested in their own comfort and gratification.

Of course there are exceptions to this, such as a spouse or a very close friend who may love us unconditionally, but this is very rare indeed. We should be thankful for the people who are in our lives, for without people to share our lives with, life is quite meaningless. But it is dangerous to look to them to validate us as a human being. If a person looks to other human beings to estimate their worth, they will live a life that is simply a whirlwind of reactions formulated to win the approval of others, which then opens them to all sorts of manipulations by other people. It is better to be like a thermostat rather than a thermometer. A thermometer simply fluctuates to whatever the temperature in the room happens to be, whereas a thermostat determines the temperature in a given space. Our own validation of our personal identity and God-given value should be strong enough within us at our heart level that we never need to depend on outside influences to help us feel better about ourselves.

In fact, a person could have the best people in the world as friends and associates, but it is "what we know" that will determine whether those great people will want to continue to hang around us! Also, "what you know" will, to a great extent, determine what specific people are going to initially be attracted to you in life.

The kind of charisma that we exude is also greatly affected by "what we do or don't know." If we know the truth about ourselves and the truth that God's intention for us is always good, ("For I know the plans I have for you, says the Lord. They are plans for good and not for evil, to give you a future and a hope." Jeremiah 29:11) we will exude a kind of charisma that will draw good, honest, wonderful, and successful people to us.

On the other hand, if "what we know" is that we will never get very far in life unless someone comes along to give us a lucky break, then that belief pattern will produce a "needy" type of charisma in us, and when people get around us, they will feel like we are a leach who is about to latch on to their arm and drain the life out of them.

Our personal charisma is very much like an odor in the air. I'm sure that you have had the experience of stopping at a gas station to put gas in your car, and as you are pumping the gas, you get a huge whiff of gas fumes up your nose. Those gas fumes floated up in the ether between the gas tank opening and your nose, and when you breathed those fumes into your lungs, you may have gotten lightheaded or dizzy for a moment.

I took my wife, Julie, and my four children to the movie theater last weekend, and I experienced a phenomenon that you may also be familiar with. I call it the "Magnetic Popcorn Affect." Before going to the theater, I had just taken my whole family out for dinner, and even though everyone was already full by the end of the meal, somehow we also found some room for dessert. The restaurant was about a one-minute drive from the movie theater, so knowing that we didn't have far to drive, we got in the car and arrived at the theater only two or three minutes before the movie was about to start. After we got our tickets, we started walking through the lobby, and before we could get into the theater, we were encountered by something very strong in the ether waves of the lobby. All at once we were overcome by the smell of fresh buttery popcorn filling the air. Obviously, none of us had a legitimate need for food because we had just stuffed ourselves at the restaurant minutes before, but can you guess what our collective reaction was as we passed the concession stand? You guessed right! We all agreed that the popcorn smelled so good that we had to get some to take into the movie theater with us!

Most of us have also had the experience of being gone from home for a few days but when we return, we go into the kitchen and open the refrigerator and WHAM...this smell hits us in the face, and we know that some food is beginning to rot.

Much like the reaction that a person has to this sense of physical smell, the charisma that you or I are exuding is either attracting or repelling people as we interact with them during our daily lives.

Some people may be keeping their positivity a secret

If we are exuding the right kind of attractive charisma and a person still does not react to us as positively as we would like, there is the possibility that they may be hiding their positivity until they get to know us better. Even if a person likes what we are saying, they could still be wondering if it sounds too good to be true or if we can actually

although prospect may be positive but
he still wants to know what we are
offering is actually worthwhile for them

14

They want something concrete for them to have trust in us. Maybe somebody

carry through with our part of whatever we are proposing to them. *promised them something and they under delivered.*

To a great extent we can't blame people for having a certain amount of caution. We have all been disappointed in the past by someone who has over-promised something to us and then under-delivered. So we should be willing to allow people to spend a little time "checking us out" before they allow us to earn their trust. *Leaders come early and stay late, they always put in*

I have been privileged to serve in a leadership position of one type or another for more than thirty years. I believe that true leaders are always expanding their vision and moving into new territory. *the extra effort to be servers to their followers.*

We can see in the very meaning of the title "leaders" that these are people who will go before and stay at least one step ahead of the people who are following them. If we are at least one step ahead of the people who are following us, we can teach them how to take that next step. Now, it is much better to be ten or twenty steps ahead of the people we are mentoring, but even if we are only one or two steps ahead in our progress, we can still qualify as a leader. Someone once said, *"You can't teach what you don't know, and you can't lead where you don't go"! Leaders are Role model to their followers,*

Great leaders who want the best for their protégées are constantly working to sell people on ideas that will help them improve their personal and or professional lives. The best and most healthy order is for every leader to also have a leader as a mentor and role model. To be assured of the strongest foundation of leadership, we all need some amount of accountability, and the highest and best structure is when leaders are people who follow leaders, who follow leaders, who follow leaders…

With a passion to go to the next higher level and to help others do the same, leaders are always involved in *Upline always wants their downline to grow. They want* 15 *you to move to the next level.*

People usually do not get it the 1st 2nd + then the 3rd Time

the pursuit of helping other individuals expand their thinking. In this context, I will make a couple of brief statements here and later will go into more detail. **In my experience over the years, most of the greatest people I have had the privilege to work with did not respond to me in an overwhelmingly positive way the first, second, or often the third time I encountered them. Also, many of the best business deals I have been blessed with came after what seemed like several rejections, and in some cases, after many interactions that ended in a way which left me wondering if the person I was talking with had any real interest at all in what I was proposing to them!**

The important thing is how you

The fact that we seem to be rejected personally or that our vision, mission, idea, or business opportunity seems to have been rejected is nowhere near as important as how we react to that perceived rejection. *react to their rejection.*

I believe from the bottom of my heart that **people should be required to get our permission before they are given the privilege of rejecting us.** We should grant them this permission to reject us only after we have fully qualified them and have decided that they are not supposed to be a part of the vision, mission, or business that we are building. After this qualifying process is complete, if we determine that they are not a person whom we are purposed to work with, then we can simply release them to go and find where they do fit--with someone else at some other location on the planet. But it is important to not release people before we have first fully qualified them. Once you dig a little deeper to find out who they really are and you take the time to allow them to see who you really are, the whole dynamic of your interactions with them can make a dramatic shift. We may not always see it at first glance, but as we go beyond the surface image, we can find the people who will become our best friends and or most valued associates! *As we know more about people we associate they could be our best friends or Valued Associates*

16

Overcoming does not mean that one won the contest and the other person lost means in this book

Overcoming

In the title of this book I used the word "overcoming." This word means different things to different people. So let's agree on a specific definition in context with the message contained in the pages of this book.

When the average person hears or sees the word overcome, he or she could assume it means that there was some type of conquest and that one person won the battle and another person lost. Naturally in this type of interaction it would be assumed that the person who won would be crowned the "overcomer" and the other person would be labeled the "loser." While this scenario is played out continually in every day life, this <u>is not</u> the meaning of the word "overcoming" in the context of this book.

The truth about rejection is that it is not inevitably permanent, and it is often only a knee-jerk reaction on the part of the other person. If you continue to talk to people with "relaxed intensity," you will feel less of a need for them to say yes to you immediately. **"Relaxed intensity" is a total knowing in your heart of hearts that you are on purpose and that you are just sorting through people to find the specific individuals who you were meant to be with all along.** *When you STP often then you don't have to think of what you have*

It is also important that we learn the art of "mastering the mundane". **"Mastering the mundane" is the ability to say the same exact words and paint the same exact picture of your vision or opportunity hundreds, or even thousands, of times to different people and still keep your strong passion and deep conviction flowing with every word that you speak.** You may have said those same exact words so many times that you don't even have to think about what you are going to say anymore. This is when you can put your full concentration on creating the great-

to say it comes Naturally. Its like a piano player or guitarist or dancer who has performed several times & who has

est possible dynamics in your presentation. It is similar to a guitarist who has played a song so many times that she or he no longer has to think about the chord or next note to be played or like a dancer who has perfected a dance routine to the point where she no longer has to consciously order the next step to take. It simply comes as a natural flow. It is at this point of "mastering the mundane" that they can fully concentrate on maximizing their creative expression and charisma. *perfected his dance does not have to worry of what steps*

As we pay the price to develop genuine "relaxed intensity" and to "master the mundane," we will have the freedom of mind and heart to read even the most subtle nuances of a person's reaction to our presentation, and if we need to, we will be able to switch our approach at a second's notice. *the needs to take on a piano player a guitarist does not*

When we are free from being preoccupied with what we need to say, then we will be more sensitive and better able to identify and address the issues that the individual is most interested in or conflicted about. When we are free to observe the more subtle nuances of human interaction, we find that much of the time what we first thought to be a rejection or a red stoplight was really just a yellow caution light, indicating that we needed to adjust our approach to better fit that specific person. *worry about the next note. It comes natural.*

Too often people plow ahead in a conversation with a feeling that they need to "get their point across," without giving the person they are talking with an adequate opportunity to supply valuable feedback. God gave us two ears and one mouth, so at times it makes sense that listening might be more important than talking. Being a genuinely interested listener will make us a good steward of our time and theirs. It might be better to continue the conversation on another day because they have already had too many pressures that day and are mentally and *Then we have the Heart & Mind to adjust to a person's Reaction & But*

people sometimes want to get their point across without valuable feedback from

emotionally running on overload. To give them any more *people* to think about would only be defeating our purpose. *If you stay relaxed + let the prospect know*

Whatever the specific reasons are that may cause a *or* delay, **if you can hang in there and stay relaxed with just** *feel* **enough intensity to let the other person feel your passion, you will often find that your persistence will finally intersect with the right timing in their life.** When the timing is right, it is not uncommon for what seemed like a big NO to suddenly turn into a big YES. I can speak from much personal experience that a door that seems to be shut and locked can suddenly swing wide open. *your passion.*

You've gone enough round the prospect

Very often, the bigger the benefits are that you will eventually reap from establishing a connection, the more important the issue of timing is with respect to finally having the door of opportunity open for you. You don't have to win them all; you just have to win the most important ones. And many of the most important ones are just in a holding pattern for a period of time. When you have finally tried enough different approaches, you will eventually land on something that hits their "hot button". *Show interest in them and connecting with them*

The meaning of the word OVERCOMING in the context of the title and content of this book is simply the *"the act of rising above or to transcend"* the undesirable reactions that are unleashed or directed toward us from other people. *will help.*

Three reactions to perceived rejection: *is also something we feel that what we said was not*

1- We can *be overcome* by a perceived rejection and assume that the other person is right and we are wrong. This causes us to lose our self-esteem and conclude that we probably weren't very good at explaining what we shared with them, or we may even begin to believe that our ideas are worthless and it was pointless to bother explaining our vision or opportunity to this person to begin with. *Right + we were wrong. This will lower our self esteem + make us feel that we did not explain things properly.*

When we defend our position + try to win them over, we are actually pushing them further away from us.

2- We can _resist_ or fight the perceived rejection. We can try to present a case of why we are right and they are wrong, which usually results in someone becoming defensive. When we begin to defend our position in the presence of someone who has offered us some form of resistance, we will often find that even though we may be trying to give them affirming reasons to win them over to our way of thinking, in reality we only end up pushing them farther away. If we become defensive and then they respond to us with a defensive stance, it will become increasingly difficult to reach any kind of positive outcome. *In this way we may not be able to make a positive outcome*

3- We can _Overcome or Rise Above_ the perceived rejection by going higher, to the level where the truth is. *We are not looking for everyone to say yes.*

   a. We need to be totally convinced in our heart of hearts of *the truth* that the vision or opportunity we are presenting is so valuable that our passion for this vision has caused us to go beyond the point of no return. We are not going to ever stop sharing our vision with others and this 100% commitment has now put us on a mission to share our vision for freedom with as many people as possible. Whether any one specific person reacts positively or negatively to our proposal will not make our vision appear more or less valuable to us, because our conviction about the great value of our vision or our opportunity is strong and replete. **Our purpose in sharing our vision or opportunity is not to have everyone like us or to have everyone say "yes" to us. Our purpose is to continue to share our vision so that we can find those select individuals who are meant to become our associates, which will result in a connection that takes place at a heart level between us and those specific people.** *We are looking for a select few who going to run with us on the may that we run on a heart to heart level.*

Most important is to know the true Need of the people we are talking to. Knowing

b. Being able to "rise above" rejection requires that we know *the truth* about what is taking place in any interaction that we have with another person. This requires discernment. Some people have been gifted with it, and other people will have to work to learn the art of discernment. A major component of discernment is the ability to see the true needs of the people we are talking with. Discovering *the truth* about their real heartfelt needs is the best way for you to help them see the vision of what you are presenting. If they can see how the ideas you are presenting can satisfy some of their true heart-level needs, they may be able to begin to own the vision or opportunity that you are proposing to them. The benefit of having discernment is revealed when you find the number one thing that an individual believes she or he needs. The opportunity you are sharing may have many various benefits, but the important question to ask yourself is, "Which one of these benefits will be the most important one to the specific individual I am talking with at this time?" Receiving more money may be one of the benefits; more free time to spend with her family may be one of the benefits, becoming financially free, which would enable her to quit working a job that she has hated for years could be the biggest benefit in her mind. Some of the other benefits could be totally separate from finances. The most important benefit for an individual could be to gain positive friends to associate with. Maybe he already sees himself as being financially successful but has no time to enjoy his prosperity because he is too busy working sixteen hours a day, and every time his cell phone rings, his stomach gets tied up in knots because it may be a call telling him he needs to drop what he is doing

More Money time with family. Financial freedom. Leave the 21/6 hrs Job she has.

To find out the true needs, we need to ask Questions, Pay attention and LISTEN with eye contact.

with his family and go back to work. The list goes on and on, but the main point here is that through discernment we are able to zero in on the one main need of the person we are talking with. How do we do this zeroing in process? We ask questions, and then giving our full attention, we shut our mouth and we listen. I know this can be difficult to do, especially when we have the passion and purpose of what we want to say making our heart almost beat out of our chest, but asking questions and listening is the main way to get our discernment to kick into gear. We can ask questions like "If you could redesign your life any way that you desired, what would your best possible life be like for you?" or "In what areas of your life would you like to experience a higher level of freedom and a lower level of stress?" By asking people questions about their jobs, their family, their goals, their dreams for the future, and so forth...if we listen closely, we can find the one biggest need that they have. If they are underpaid and overworked at their present job and are in debt up to their eyeballs, then *the truth* about their number one need could be that they sense a strong need to make more money and secure a stronger financial future for them and their family. If this is their strongest need, then you can simply show them *the truth* about how they can fulfill that financial need by working with you and your vision. For the people who feel they already have enough money but their job controls them sixteen hours a day, you can show them how by working with you they could possibly make just as much money but leverage their time more wisely and have more time to spend doing other things they enjoy. For another person, the greatest need that could be filled by working with

0

LISTEN ②

ASK ③

FORM

④

GOOD PROGRAM

① more money

② family

③ Enough money NO time

leverage Time

you is that she would become more centered and stronger spiritually by being under your mentorship. Another individual may have never really felt connected to his parents or family members, so the greatest immediate need is to establish a sense of "belonging somewhere". You and your other associates may become, in a sense, the family that person never had before. It is not uncommon for a protégée to see his or her mentor as the father or mother they wished they had been blessed with in their early years. Now, here you are, and you are like a dad or a mom to her or maybe like the sister or brother he always wished he'd had. Knowing *the truth* about the other person's greatest need and desire puts you in a place where you can help that individual make a shift to her next higher level, and *the truth* is the fuel that she will need to propel herself higher. If a person's number one need is to have more money, then he may not be inspired by talk about all the great relationships he will be able to develop with those he will be working with. When you know the truth about an individual's greatest need, that truth will set you free to help him or her to move forward in life. It is amazing to see the reaction on people's faces when you finally narrow things down to their greatest need and then you explain how the vision or opportunity that you are presenting to them will meet, or maybe even surpass, their greatest need. Even if they seemed disconnected or bewildered before you hit the hot button of their greatest need, after you hit the bull's-eye, it is not uncommon for people to say something like, "Oh, now I see what you are talking about!!!" All that really happened here is that you guided these people through the fog of their undefined perception of life and helped them to focus on *the truth* about what they really wanted out of life, and then you showed them how they could achieve the very thing they believed they wanted most. Whatever people think they need more of is what you show them how to achieve. It is a wonderful thing to behold when you have helped a person get to the heart of the matter and get up to the thought level where he or she can see *the truth* that what you are presenting to them will help them fulfill their desires and dreams. At that point in time that person is transported to a higher level where *the truth* lives and all of the rejection is left behind on the lower level from which they departed! "When you know the truth, (in any area of life) the truth will make you free" This works spiritually, mentally, in relationships, financially, and yes, this principle even works in overcoming and rising above rejection!

I cannot count the number of times when I have been on a plane flying from one place to another, and in mid-flight, I hear the pilot on the pubic address system telling us that we have encountered some turbulence, and they are going to move the plane up to a higher altitude to find a place where we will have a smoother ride. This is the same idea we are talking about here, only instead of going an actual number of feet higher above the earth, we are going to a higher altitude of truth-based thoughts.

What we are looking for is the altitude that coincides with the real truth about the person we are interacting with at the moment. A pilot will either go to a higher altitude to get out of the turbulence or will go to a lower altitude where the turbulence does not exist. In this same way as we are looking for the 'truth level' in any given conversation or negotiation, sometimes the "truth level" is above where the other person is coming from, and sometimes the "truth level" is at a lower altitude than where the other person is coming from. But either way we always get the conversation on a higher quality level when we can get the interaction on the level of being totally real.

For example, there are times during our interaction with people when they are negative in their thinking and we need to take the level of conversation to a higher level in order to get the conversation to the level of truth or to "the way it really is" in context with the topic that we are discussing. At other times the person we are talking with is so puffed up with an over-inflated ego that the only way to get the conversation to the truth level is for us to actually bring the conversation to what may seem to be a lower altitude than the synthetic, imaginary level that the other person thinks they are operating on.

There are some principles that seem to work in a much different way than the average person would assume. For example: "The greatest amongst you will be the servant," or "The one who takes the lowest place will be exalted to the highest place," or "The first shall be last, and the last shall be first," or one of my favorites, "The meek shall inherit the earth." These principles are confusing to some people, especially if they are used to trying to force things to happen in their life.

When you get on the level of the truth and "the way it really is," you become like the cream that always rises to the top. At first it may appear that we are taking a lower place, but when all the fog clears, we see that what we really did was step down onto an elevator that took us to the top floor!

I am sure that you have dealt with people whose image of themselves is nothing more than a well-orchestrated illusion. With smoke and mirrors they try to convince the people around them that they somehow are better and smarter than the rest, and they do not feel that they have to operate in accordance with the same truth-based success principles that everyone else needs to work within in order to create legitimate success.

If the person we are dealing with is attempting to impress us with a deceptive act of trying to make us believe that they are "the best thing since sliced bread," often the best thing to do is to actually get underneath that person's ego and take an even more humble stance than usual.

If someone is bouncing off the walls, telling you how great they are, they are usually doing so because they feel insecure. Of course they may be trying their best to not let their insecurity show, so they may proceed to put on a song and dance to try to get you to believe that "they are the greatest and everything is simply wonderful."

As we gently bring the conversation down a notch or two, we will be able to support that person in their frail, precarious state. They are "walking the high wire of their ego." To support them we must first help them down from the tightrope on which they are walking before they fall and get hurt. This is often a good time to be as calm as you can, and it is usually best for you to lower your voice and try to guide this individual to a level that is more truth based in context with the greatness of 'who they really are'. The great result that occurs when we help a person do this is they end up seeing that who they 'really are' is actually more wonderful than who they were pretending to be!

I will discuss this technique in more detail later in this book, but for now we will just relate to this in the context of the "getting out of the turbulence" metaphor.

When communicating with people, it is also good to

work to keep the interaction on a healthy emotional pitch. Depending on the person you are dealing with, sometimes you need to take the conversation higher and sometimes you need to take it to a lower emotional pitch in order to get that person "out of the turbulence" and on to the truth.

Even when we have to lower the emotional pitch of the conversation, we are not lowering the quality or the truth level, we are simply helping the person to lower their misguided balloon before it floats too high up into the atmosphere and pops from the intense pressure of the facade they are trying to keep afloat. Our objective in this type of interaction is never to try to prove who is right or who is wrong, but rather what is right and what is the solid truth foundation to build on. "When we know the truth, the truth sets us free." Truth is always our objective.

Just about every thing in life is one type of negotiation or another. As we negotiate with people throughout life, many of these people will be driven by insecurity, feelings of unworthiness, fears, and all kinds of other debilitating problems. Others that we deal with will be coming from a place of truth- based principled thinking.

A great part of the premise for this book is to overcome rejection by shifting our thinking to a higher level than the person who is either resisting or rejecting us. By shifting our thinking to a higher level we can rise above the smoke screen of their excuses, which often have little or no foundation of truth.

The truth is always on a higher level than the excuses that people come up with. Excuses are one of the favorite techniques people use when they are trying to avoid committing to any idea or plan that will improve their lives.

Take the high road

The trick here is for us to stay out of the emotional trap being laid for us when a person is using excuses or any other technique to reject us or the ideas we are proposing to them. If we take it as a personal insult and our emotions start to go wild and our mind shifts into the "justify our position" mode, look out…because sparks, and maybe even verbal bullets, are about to fly, and any hope of a positive outcome is probably about to fly right out the window.

When we go into a conversation with another person or a group of people, we need to take the high road and have it already preset in our mind and heart that we are going to put all of our thought, creativity, and emotional energy into keeping the conversation 100% real. . This will bring a freedom and a depth to the interaction like nothing else can.

Before we endeavor to present ideas, a vision, or even a business proposal to other people, it is imperative that we have already established within ourselves a strong faith in that idea, vision, or business. It is most likely that we do have a strong belief in our vision, mission, or ideas or we probably would not take the time and to go through all the work necessary in order to present this to another person. However, often the truth about why your idea, vision, or business opportunity has great value can be lost in the emotional tug of war that ensues once the other person detects that what you are sharing will require a thoughtful response and an eventual commitment on their part.

One way for a person to attempt to avoid appearing uninformed is to resist you with the first thing that flies through his mind. It's often not even a real reason; it's just the best thing that he could come up with on the spur of the moment.

I am sure that you have had conversations with people

who seemed to be on a different planet while you were endeavoring to talk with them. You can almost hear the wheels turning in their head as they are totally preoccupied with searching their brain to think up the most impressive response to blurt out as soon as you finish your sentence. With this type of people it is obvious we have to assume that they are not going to hear much of what we are saying because the high volume of their personal thoughts make it impossible for them to hear most of our words. If you find a person like this, and you believe that you are meant to work together, you have to be prepared to talk with them several times before they will really start to hear what you are saying. Once this type of person feels more comfortable being around you, she will often not feel such a strong need to outwardly impress you and therefore be more able to fully hear what you are sharing with her.

Their perception determines 'how' they will hear and see you

I have explained the principle of Thought-replacement and Thought-exchange in my other books at great length in context with our personal self-talk, and also changing our personal thoughts from negative to positive or from false-based thoughts to truth-based thoughts on a daily basis.

At certain times in this book I will touch on the subject of Thought-replacement and Thought-exchange but in this book I will deal with this subject in context with helping other people to change their thoughts.

In order to help people to stop using the knee-jerk reaction of rejection as a shield that provides them with a synthetic sense of feeling more in control and less vulnerable, we must first help them grow into becoming a more positive, optimistic, and truth-based thinker.

For example, if a person has come to a place in life where

he believes that financial freedom is not possible, then we can help that person to exchange his thoughts and go from believing the false thought, *"it is supposed to be hard to make money,"* to the truth-based thought, *"If I work within the law of reciprocity, then for me, it is not supposed to be hard to make money. It is simply a matter of making sure that my dominant thoughts are on the truth and my actions are in alignment with the law of reciprocity, which states, "As you give, so shall you receive". If I can help enough other people get what they want, than I will automatically receive what I want, and as I help enough other people get to their next higher level, this will automatically propel me to my next higher level."*

It is important that we learn to live our lives in accordance with the laws which state: "As a man or woman thinketh, so they shall be" and "We are transformed by the renewing of our mind." As we lead by example, we can then help others to learn how to operate in these same laws as well.

What does this have to do with overcoming rejection? Well, one direct affect is that the more we can help people to operate according to these same truth-based principles and laws, the more they will be in one accord with us, and the possibility of dissention or rejection will be reduced greatly because they are now operating within the same principle-based belief system.

Every human being has a different perception. If there are fifty people looking at the same meal, it is very possible that they will be seeing fifty different meals. They could all be looking at a plate with the same fish, broccoli, salad, and baked potato on it, but a person who loves broccoli will see that meal differently from a person who does not like broccoli. A strict vegetarian may like most everything that they see on the plate, but may not want the fish.

People's perceptions are to a great extent determined

by their personal preferences, their past experiences and their percentage of positive self-talk vs. their percentage of negative self-talk concerning anything they may be seeing, hearing, tasting, smelling, touching or thinking about at given moment. It is obvious that if they have 90% negative self-talk and 10% positive self-talk; they will probably react more skeptically or guarded. If they have 10% negative-self talk and 90% positive self-talk running through their head, they will probably be more positive and open minded.

The thing to remember concerning this point is that when people react to us, whatever a person's positive vs. negative thought ratio is, it was already that way before we ever encountered them. They have been collecting positive and negative thoughts for their entire life, and everyone has collected their own unique version of a thought-based reality. Therefore it is important to keep in mind that *how* any one individual is hearing and perceiving us, or what we are saying, will be determined by what thoughts they have previously collected about life, about people, about freedom, about business, about money, about work, about family, about society and about hundreds or thousands of other factors and different areas of life.

Just like the example of the plate of food being perceived differently by different people, you and I could explain the same opportunity or vision to fifty different people, and as they all look at the same "plate" of ideas that we have set before them, each person will see what is on the plate through the filter of their positive vs. negative self-talk ratio.

So rather than focusing on whether a person is going to say yes or no to us during our first encounter with them, it makes more sense to put our focus on helping individuals to feel good about themselves while they are with us and prompting them to be actively involved in the conversation rather than us just steamrolling them with a lot of information.

Understanding that this positive vs. negative self-talk based perception is always going to be different with each unique person we encounter will help us to not "take it personally" whether a person reacts positively or negatively to us at first. It is not important that they think we are a super duper genius, but it is vitally important that we have thoroughly "taken their temperature" and have found out where they are coming from mentally, emotionally and at a heart level. The greatest doctors are not the ones who try to impress their patients with their vast medical knowledge. The greatest doctors are the ones who have the wisdom to ask the right questions and do the right tests to diagnose accurately a person's problem so that they can then prescribe an effective cure.

Their perception will improve
as you help them improve their thoughts

I have mentioned a statistic in some of my CD programs and books that reveals the quality of the average person's thoughts on a daily basis. I believe it will be very enlightening for us to revisit this statistic at this point in context with overcoming rejection. This statistic also shows how the thoughts that other people are thinking while we're talking with them about a vision or opportunity very much affects their reactions to us.

After conducting tests with thousands of people, psychologists and psychiatrists have determined that 87% of the average person's self-talk is negative on a daily basis and that the average person thinks between 40,000 to 50,000 thoughts per day.

In context with overcoming rejection, I believe this is something we need to keep in mind while we are talking with new people about our vision, opportunity, product, or the service that we are proposing to them.

This means that out of the 40,000 to 50,000 thoughts that are swimming around in the head of the average person every day, between 34,800 to 43,500 of those thoughts are negative. So again we have to realize that if the average person's reaction to us is anything less than positive, it very often has nothing to do with us, but rather is based on an overload of negative thoughts they were already operating with before we ever showed up in their space. Since they were already wallowing around in their 87% negative self-talk mental-cesspool condition before we ever contacted them, it makes perfect sense to conclude that their response to us often may not even be remotely connected to the words that we spoke to them or to the reality of who we are as a human being. Helping people to begin to think more positive thoughts about life in general and the freedom that they were born to enjoy as human beings is a major key to helping them to create positive breakthroughs in their lives.

To a great extent, this has to do with our becoming leaders who know how to guide people in the right direction without them ever knowing that we knew they were heading in the wrong direction! What we are talking about here is helping people to overcome their insecurities while never letting them know that we could see they were insecure and helping people overcome thoughts of fear and unworthiness without causing them to feel embarrassed or ashamed in the possess.

These are leadership skills which I cover at great length in my 12 CD leadership audio series entitled "Breakthrough Leadership". If within these pages I explained all of these specific mentoring concepts and techniques that you can use, this book would end up being 500 or 600 pages long, so I'm not going to do that here.

But for right now let's just focus in on the fact that the more you or I can help people become more positive on the inside, the more positive their outer responses will be.

Also, the more that you and I help people to feel an increased sense of safety and security when they are in our presence, the more they will react positively to us and to the vision, opportunity, or ideas we are presenting to them. When it is clear to them that our motives are right and that we only desire good for them, then they can breathe a sigh of relief and be assured that we are not going to try to manipulate them in any way

Helping people to rid themselves of negative self-talk and helping them to increase their truth-based principle-talk is a major factor in creating unity of purpose, unity of vision, and unity of mind. This all starts with the first phone call or the first meeting where we give a person the first dose of our faith-filled charisma, our principle-based vision, and our purpose-driven ideas.

During the first exposure that we have with a new prospect who we discern has a high level of negative self-talk, it is often wise to be upfront and tell that person we are just going to give him some ideas to think about and we can get together later to discuss the ideas, vision, or business proposal in more detail. This will keep the meeting brief enough for us to plant a few positive thoughts and to end the meeting on a high note. Giving "87% negative self-talk people" too much information during the first meeting can be a bit dangerous. If we overload them with too much information some of these folks' negativity will show up in the classic defensive reactions of "No, that won't work for me," or "I had a cousin or sister who tried that, and they lost a lot of money," or "I could never be a success at anything." On the other side of the coin, there are other "87% negative self-talk people" who take the "I already know it all" approach. If you give too much information during your first meeting with "I already know it all" people, they may very presumptively tell you that they already know everything about what you are proposing, and they may even tell you that they know a better way to do it and can give you a shortcut to improve on the plan you just proposed to them!!!!

All kinds of strange things can happen during the first encounter, but don't let them throw you off track. If you feel resistance from a person during the first conversation with them and you perceive their reaction to be some sort of a rejection, this is never the time to try to overcome them with the force of your best persuasion and treat them as an adversary that needs to be subdued and tamed.

This is the time to "rise above" their undesirable reaction with something that will put them at ease and take them off their defenses. Possibly you might even want to be a little vulnerable at this point and let them know that at the beginning you also had a lot of doubts. It might be good to list the doubts you had when you were in the place that they are now in.

Of course a main key here is to never mention a doubt that you had if you still have that doubt now, because you will want to be able to give a truth-based, crystal clear answer to dissolve every doubt on your list.

If you list a number of doubts you had at the beginning of your pursuit and then you proceed to dissolve them, you may find that with each doubt you dissolve, the more disarmed the person that you are talking with will become.

This is also called the "Feel, Felt, Found Approach". You can respond to any objection by simply saying, "You know, I know exactly how you FEEL. When I first was thinking about this opportunity or this vision that I am sharing with you, I FELT the same way, but here is what I have FOUND." Then you proceed to share with them the new information or inspiration that was effective in dissolving that specific doubt and removed that skeptical point from your thought process.

This approach is also called "redirection." You are using the fact that they raised some doubts about what you are sharing as a perfect opportunity to talk about the doubts that you had at the beginning, and this provides the perfect segue for you to get the conversation out of the negative zone and back onto the highway of truth or "the way it really is." By "redirecting" you took the conversation to a higher level of truth without the need for conflict. Also, by redirecting the conversation, you were able to refocus the other person's attention away from her present doubts and get her thinking instead about your past doubts and the truth that helped you delete those doubts. This technique has a wonderful way of helping the person who is listening to feel okay about having doubts, and you are also reinforcing the fact that you value and respect their desire to know more.

Being Rich

Rising to a higher level where rejection cannot touch us also necessitates that we see "Being Rich" in a broader, truer, sense than the definition most commonly accepted as the worldwide stereotype.

If people think or feel that our only goal in dealing with them is to get more money, the result, in most cases, will be immediate rejection

It is important that we define the full scope of what it means to be RICH.

The word "rich" is also in the title of this book. The connection between being rich and overcoming rejection is very strong. If you can live with the right mindset, you will be able to overcome different types of perceived rejections on a daily basis, and yes, it is true that this is a major key to your becoming financially wealthy beyond your wildest dreams.

But the greatest benefit of being financially rich goes far beyond the actual things and the wonderful lifestyle that money can buy. **The greatest benefit of having lots of money is when you come to the place where you no longer have to worry about money!!** This occurs when you cross the line of having more than enough financial income to provide you with the lifestyle that you desire. When your income exceeds the amount of money that you need...**you are free** from having to worry about how you will get enough money to pay the bills, take a vacation, pay for college for your children, buy a new car, give to your favorite charities, etc. Many people worry about money every single day of their lives. Becoming free from having to worry about money liberates you to be able to focus your mental, emotional, and spiritual energy on the things that are really most important in your spiritual life, your family, your purpose, being creative, being a giving person, and enjoying all the blessings that are available to you here on God's good earth.

Many people will respond very positively if we ask them if they would like to become financially free, yet sometimes the same people will respond skeptically to the idea of their "becoming rich". The main reason for this is because most people have already rejected the possibility that they could ever be rich in the worldwide stereotypical sense. But if you ask any person, "Would you like to get out of debt and earn more money than you need to pay the bills each month?" the answer would inevitably be "Yes" from most people.

Money is only part of the equation, and in fact it is not the most important aspect of "Being Rich". Being able to overcome perceived rejections and getting past the often uncomfortable beginning stage of a relationship is also very important in order to develop *rich relationships* that will stand the test of time and adversity. Some of the most solid, valued relationships that grow stronger and stronger over the years do not necessarily start out that way.

In fact, some of the people who are our closest friends and associates today may not have impressed us, or we may not have impressed them, very much the first or second time we were with them. At first there may have been a bit of awkwardness, and this may have created many questions in your mind and in their minds as well. Some of these questions many have caused either you or them to put a guard up until you could get beneath the surface of your personalities.

Until two people can truly trust each other, it is very natural for them to be somewhat guarded. This being guarded and not totally opening yourself up to another person, or them not totally being open with you, can, at times feel very much like rejection, even though it is not really rejection at all. It is simply the feeling of not being completely sure about the other person.

Overcoming rejection also makes us **rich in peace.** When we no longer have to deal with the inner turmoil of having to be preoccupied with other people's opinions of us, a sense of peace, calm, and confidence comes to our life. It is a fact that many, if not most people. are so focused on gaining the approval of other people that they live each day with the stress of trying to act, look, sound, and be like they think everyone wants them to be. This way of living causes a person to lose their unique identity, and they become a robot that hopes people will like them. Even if people do seem to like their façade, they still can never be quite sure if people would like who they really are. They are conflicted with the knowledge that they are putting on an act. This is a very stressful way to live. When we are no longer controlled by whether people accept us or reject us, this is a major step toward living a life filled with peace.

Overcoming rejection enhances every area of our lives. If we sum it up in one word, the greatest manifestation of living **a rich life** is **<u>freedom</u>**. Freedom in our spiritual life, our family life, our financial prosperity, our purpose, our ability to be a blessing to others, our friendships, our mental and emotional state, our physical health and energy, and the list goes on and on and on…

The more free we become, the richer we are!

Know that you have a great purpose

To rise to a higher level where rejection can't touch you, you must also know that you showed up here on this round ball in space with a great destiny to fulfill. You were born for a great purpose and to fulfill a wonderful vision to live throughout your life here on earth. Not one person was dropped on this planet by accident. Not one person was dropped on this planet without a great purpose to fulfill. God has created each of us with a specific plan to follow and manifest. You were created in the image and likeness of God, and you already have all the equipment necessary to fulfill your purpose and your mission. The art of living is to learn to use the equipment that we have been given to its greatest effectiveness.

Other people may not be able to see the value of your purpose or identify with "where you are coming from," but that's okay. They don't need to! They need to be on a pursuit of their own God-given purpose. So if your purpose doesn't line up with theirs, and their vision seems to be out of alignment with yours, don't worry about it. There are several billion other people on the planet who are possibilities for you to work with!

Trust Your Inner Guidance System

Finally, rising to a higher level where rejection can't touch you is best achieved by simply being natural and being your true self. Know that you are special. Walk like you are in a mission for good. Talk with the deep conviction of a pure heart. Be true to your purpose for freedom. And trust that you are fulfilling your God given destiny.

When you know that you are "on purpose" you will also know that you can trust the inner guidance system that works very naturally when you are purpose-driven and you have your heart in the right place.

I remember very clearly a January flight to Salt Lake City, Utah. We were about to land at the Salt Lake City airport when the pilot came on the intercom with an announcement. He said, "Good evening. If you look out of your window, you will notice that all you can see is thick fog. Well, fortunately this jet is equipped with instruments that will allow us to land this plane without having to see the ground. The instruments are so accurate and sophisticated that the plane can land itself with zero visibility." Then he added, "Friends, there are dozens of planes that are circling this airport right now, and if the fog does not clear, they will have to be rerouted to another airport so that they don't run out of fuel. You are flying on one of the few select jets that will be able to land at the Salt Lake City airport tonight."

Just like that jet, we have a built-in guidance system.

Many people avoid landing on anything specific in life because they don't believe they will have the inner knowing and guidance that they will need to be able to keep running with the vision they have been fantasizing about. Often these are the same people who will stop working to go to their next higher level because they don't like the feeling of being rejected. But I believe everyone has an inner guidance system that will let them know that they can be a victor instead of a victim and that freedom is within their reach.

When you know...that you know...that you know... that the vision you are building is your "lot in life'" and the destiny that you were born to fulfill, you will also know that you have been provided with the necessary inner guidance system you will need to navigate your-self to higher and higher levels of success. So STEP OUT THERE AND MAKE IT HAPPEN. You have what it takes, and you have the inner equipment to land right on your dream and make it a reality

Chapter

2

Be an Icebreaker

If you and I are going to constantly broaden our sphere of influence and therefore expand our vision into greater success, we are going to have a lot of encounters with people in which we will have to break through the icy exterior of their protective shell before any valuable communication can take place. Depending on how thick that ice is, some individuals may need to bask in the warmth of our charisma for a period of time so that the ice will melt and become thin enough for us to break. You and I will personally grow stronger with each successful ice-breaking experience. Our ability to not be put off every time we run into something that feels like rejection will result in our having the collective experiential wisdom to look beyond the first encounter we have with people and take the time to look deeper into who they really are.

There is no doubt that many people miss out on some of the greatest relationships because they are too touchy and run away at the first sign of discomfort or anything less than total approval.

We have to have an extra durable layer of "thick skin" if we are going to have the opportunity to be with strong successful people, because they will challenge us and cause us to stretch.

When we are first "Breaking the Ice" to connect with a

person it is very possible that when the other person questions us about whatever we are proposing, even <u>though our first reaction might be to feel rejected, the fact may be that this is actually a genuine sign of interest on that individual's part.</u>

After two or three meetings or phone conversations we may get past the awkward feelings and "break the ice," and twenty years later we could be in a strong trusting personal or business relationship with this individual. In hindsight it is amazing to see what we may have missed out on if we, through insecurity, had misread people and wrote them off too quickly.

Stay emotionally free from other people's opinions of you

One of the automatic benefits that we gain while overcoming rejection and learning to be a great "ice breaker" is an increased sense of worthiness and confidence. Every time we take a cold encounter with someone and turn it into a warm conversation, we ourselves become more emotionally rich. **You are rich emotionally when you have a strong enough sense of confidence that you are no longer worried about what other people think about you.** Being free from worry about other people's opinions of you is a beautiful thing!

Just think of all the time and energy people put into worrying about how others are rating them. Many people live the majority of their day trying to "fix themselves up," believing that somehow this will make them more worthy and acceptable.

When we become emotionally free in relationships, we are free from having to perform to win the approval of others.

In truth, we can get to the place where we don't care what other people think about us. I'm not talking about flipping people off and being arrogant. That is definitely not what I'm talking about here. In fact, truth-based purpose-driven people who are truly free from the opinions of others are people who operate with a great sense of humility because they realize that the foundation of their self worth comes from the fact that God created them in His image and after His likeness. When you truly know that the greatness within you is a gift from God, a natural humility comes with that knowledge. You know that with God all things are possible and that without God, we are nothing. Each moment our heart keeps beating is a gift from God; each time we take another breath of air is a gift. The dream to have freedom in every area of our lives is a desire that has been placed in every women and every man by God, and if this desire for freedom was not imparted to us, we would not be able to comprehend what freedom is, let alone be able to believe that freedom is possible for us!

Neutralizing Rejection

We often perceive that people have rejected us because we sense disapproval or dissatisfaction on their part. However, *all feelings of dissatisfaction concerning another person's reaction to us or a circumstance that has occurred is simply our opinion that the outcome is undesirable.*

It was 6:15 AM when I awoke and looked out the window. Snow was billowing down in a winter blizzard with a temperature of 4 degrees Fahrenheit, which was equal to15 degrees below zero when factoring in the gusty wind chill. I thought to myself, "I wish it was warm and sunny." I felt frustrated that the weather was not more like I wanted it to be. There was nothing wrong with the weather. It was just the way it often is on a winter's day in Pennsylvania. It was my perception that caused my frustration. The temperature and the snow simply contradicted my opinion that the day would be better if the weather was warmer.

We sometimes mistake a person's reaction to be a sign of rejection because that person didn't react the way we would have liked them to. In reality we are witnessing a contradiction to our desired outcome. If we can avoid the temptation to pre-determine how people should react to us, or how a situation should work out or be resolved, then we can stay detached from the outcome and detached from the feeling of frustration and the worry that "someone or something is against us" and wants to ruin our desired outcome. We can take a "no" for just what it is and not as a personal attack. We may have wanted a "yes," but we don't need a "yes" to make us feel more secure. If we have already decided beforehand that we will give it our "best shot" and that whatever happens is okay, than the onus is on the other person and not on us. I may want it to be 70 degrees and sunny outside, but if it's 4 degrees and a snow blizzard, then that's just "what it is." If I get upset because I think that the weather should be different, I am letting a contradiction of my opinion control my attitude. **IF I CAN AVOID HAVING AN OPINION ABOUT THINGS <u>THAT I CANNOT CONTROL</u>, THEN I CAN ALSO AVOID FEELING OUT OF CONTROL AND FRUSTRATED BY CONTRADICTIONS THAT I HAD NO WAY OF DETERMINING WOULD OR WOULD NOT OCCUR. WHERE THERE IS NO CONTRADICATION, THERE IS NO POTENTIAL OF FEELING REJECTED OR FRUSTRATED, AND WHERE THERE IS NO FIXED OPINION ABOUT THE THINGS WE CAN'T CONTROL, THERE WILL NEVER BE A CONTRADICTION.**

So the key here is...**never become emotionally attached to the outcome unless you can control that outcome.** If the outcome depends on other people or the weather or other factors outside of your personal control, then stay detached.

Over time we can change circumstances and we can help people to change for the better, but "the way it is" at this moment is "the way it is." We may want it to be different, but that doesn't change the fact that "the way it is" at the present time is simply "the way it is." There is a Scripture verse that says Abraham, "The Father of many nations", "Spoke of things that be not as though they were." It does **not** say that he "spoke of things that were as though they were not." We can avoid a lot of disappointments and wasted time dealing with people and circumstances by simply being real and knowing that if we have done our best, then that is all that matters, and that is really all we really had control of to begin with!

They don't have the right to reject you until they've done their homework

This applies to any vision, mission, or idea that you may be presenting for other people's consideration. Let's say, for example, that you are a person who is promoting a business opportunity. You may be sharing your vision with other people and giving them the opportunity to build their own satellite version of your business.

As you paint a picture for other people to see the benefits of joining you in business, the only rejection that you should receive that has any merit should come only after a prospect has done due diligence to study your company manual, your marketing plan, your products, etc., and understands the benefits of the business and the products inside and out. It is also essential that the prospect has been out in the field with people, working the approved system that makes the business work.

If a person has not done due diligence to study and

actively work the business system, then he or she has no right to flat out reject you or your opportunity. After doing due diligence, this person may choose to continue to work with us, or maybe they won't, but for any individual to flat out reject us without fully checking out what we are proposing, that person is simply blowing a lot of hot air. I have a lot more respect for people who are honest and simply say, "Larry, I am not in a place in life where I want to take the time to do what you are proposing to me." I may not like that response when I hear a person say that, but if that is truly where they are at in life, at least they are being honest instead of putting up some sort of smoke screen of excuses or becoming defensive.

I respect people who are honest. I had a friend say something to me recently that I really liked. He said, "I always tell the truth, because then I never have to try to remember what I said to someone. All I have to do is remember what the truth is. Life is a lot simpler that way."

As a skilled "Ice Breaker", whether we have a negative reaction to a "perceived rejection" from another person or a positive "truth principle based" reaction is really within our control. **If the option to quit building our vision, mission or business it still a possibility and we still have lots of doubts and fears then other people's reactions can easily sway us. But if we have predetermined that quitting is not an option and we are going to do whatever it takes to make our dream become a reality, other people's reactions will not have the power to stop us or even slow us down.**

I use the words "perceived rejection" because our reaction is always controlled by our perception of the experience. Whether our thoughts are on truth or in error determines the accuracy of our perception and our ability to see what the "perceived rejection" actually was, why it took place, or whether it has any legitimacy at all.

Seeing ourselves and others accurately and in accordance with "truth-based success principles" gives us the ability to evaluate and qualify each "close encounter of the rejection kind" and compare it with the standard of "the truth" or "the way it really is". This reveals what is really going on beneath and behind the "perceived rejection." As you practice the mind-set laid out in this book you will be able to neutralize the negative affects and feelings, which, in the past, may have followed a "close encounter of the rejection kind."

You will also clearly see if you need to make an adjustment to correct your rejection perception, or whether the person you are dealing with needs to make an adjustment in their thinking.

If you need to make an adjustment in your thinking, you simply reset yourself on the truth and move on. If you see that the other person needs to make an adjustment in his or her thinking, you can then try to help that person make a mind-set adjustment. If she does adjust and decides to go with the flow, you can keep flowing with her. If she refuses to make the adjustment in her thinking, then you can just politely depart from her presence so that her distorted perception does not start affecting you.

There is no need to stay around negative people until you start to feel yourself being drained, because then your truth level starts to go down. There is a phrase in the book of Proverbs that states "Guard your heart with all diligence, for out of it flows the issues of life". You can keep your thinking right on with success laws and foundational truth-principles even when you are briefly exposed to the most negative of people. But it is best to get away from these energy drainers as soon as possible.

"Guard your heart with all diligence, for out of it flows the issues of life." **When your heart is right and you have a good plan of action, along with a willingness to work relentlessly while believing in your mission with all of your heart...nothing that you are purposed to achieve will be impossible for you.**

Though at times the odds may seem to be insurmountable, though at times people may seem to be working against us, though at times the weather seems to be our adversary and delays our plans to move forward, the resilient person's perspective is to believe that somehow things will always work out. If the airport is closed due to inclement weather, then tomorrow the weather will be more favorable for the trip. The last three people to whom you have presented your vision and ideas may have not seemed the least bit interested. In fact, at times a person may have been downright rude to you, but as you read down your ever expanding list of people you will be calling in the next few days, you know that there are some real winners somewhere on that list. So you just need to keep digging until you find the gold. This is the kind of attitude that causes constant forward momentum and has a compounding, cumulative affect when carried over from one day to the next.

Anyone who continues to move forward in the face of rejection will inevitably have a breakthrough into the next higher level of their dream-purpose and the next higher level of freedom in their spiritual, mental, relational, financial, and every other area of their life.

People may misunderstand your strength

Every person who is truly living within their "God Given Greatness" will walk in genuine humility, but there is a possibility that some people will not perceive you to be humble and will at times misunderstand your purpose-driven passion as you endeavor to "break the ice". She or he may even accuse you of being self-centered. Often those who accuse you of being self centered don't like the fact that you do not fit the picture of who they think you should be.

If we do not have a strong truth-principle based foundation established in our lives, we might be shaken by the distorted opinions of others, but when we have spiritually, mentally, and emotionally come to the place where we live our lives in alignment with a truth-based principle awareness, we will have the ability to stay detached from other people's distorted thinking. Even when other people are totally focused on the outer and the superficial, if we know that we know that our true identity is who we really are on the inside, then we can live with this motto: **"Other people's opinions of me are not any of my spiritual business".**

You will find that, for the most part, judgmental people will react to your freedom with negativity. If it is possible, you can deflect their fiery darts and arrows of negativity by influencing them to think more positively. If they will not accept a more positive way of thinking you can just let their negative darts bounce off of you as you plan a quick exit, or as my mother used to say, "Let it roll off you like water off of a duck's back". **In truth, most people who have a negative reaction to us when they see us going for the next higher level of our freedom are not just reacting to us. They are also often reacting to their <u>own</u> <u>rejected dreams</u> of freedom.**

You are simply reminding them of the fact that they have settled for a lower-level comfort-zone existence. It's not your fault that they are refusing to go forward and higher in life, but many of these folks will try to make you feel guilty because you are not willing to settle for and stay on a lower level with them!

A balance of strength and humility

While we are living in a balance of strength and humility, we learn the art of being strong without being rude or arrogant. When you are flowing from the "real you," you are fulfilling your true destiny.

When dogs have babies, they have puppies; when rabbits have babies, they have bunnies; when eagles have babies they have little eaglets; and when God the Creator has children, it only makes sense that we were born to create something wonderful, because the offspring is always like unto the parent.

The "real you" is who you are on the inside. If you put your hand over your chest and say these words, "I live in here," you will feel and bear witness to this truth. You are not your physical body; you are not your mind, will, or your emotions. These are just tools that we have been given to use while we are here on earth. The real you is where your true strength is, and that is where your God-given creative ability comes from.

Now if you don't agree with me on this point, I will not be offended, but if you think about how temporary and fragile our physical bodies, our minds, our will, and emotions are, it doesn't take long to realize that the true substance of us is in the deepest place on the inside of us, in our heart of hearts. This is where we get the strength and inspiration to go the extra mile and break through perceived limitations and preconceived boundaries. Yes, when our inner dream-purpose is big enough, then the facts don't count. When the purpose is big enough and we have faith as a mustard seed, which is pure, uncontaminated faith, then we can move mountains.

There is great strength that comes from knowing we are all the offspring of the Creator and that we were born to create.

Knowing that we were born with a purpose to be free and to have a vision to help lead many other people to freedom is a very empowering way to live. However, being strong while still being enjoyable to be around is an art form. We must make sure that we are strong without lording our strength over people. There should also be a peace and calm that people feel when they are in our presence. People love to hang around strong-centered people; they feel safe in the presence of a strong person as long as that strong person has his or her ego under control.

It is also true that <u>strong purpose-driven people love to be around other strong purpose-driven people.</u> It is a delight for strong-centered people to be in the presence of other strong-centered people because they have the opportunity to relax and not worry about being drawn into energy-draining conversations.

Another reason why strong people like to be around other strong people is that they can understand the purpose-based language they are speaking. Centered, purpose-driven people talk about possibilities and vision and a mission for the future. They are willing and ready to break free from the status quo and dare to do what others think impossible. So when purpose-driven people get together, there is a flow and a deep relating that is not forced or contrived. It is simply a oneness and a rapport that people of great vision and purpose automatically have with other people of vision and purpose. They speak from their hearts and hear from their hearts and respond accordingly.

As natural as what I have just mentioned is among strong-centered people, it can feel unnatural when talking with people who are not secure and not centered.

Know where the fire exit is

Even though we do want to help as many people become free and to help them go to the highest level possible for them in life, there is no need to try to force people to change or force things to happen. Yes, persistence is necessary, and we must act with a sense of urgency every day and with a passion to help lead people forward. But it is also vital that we know where the fire exit is so that we know how to get out of there if the conversation becomes energy draining or toxic. Some of these energy-draining people may be family members or neighbors. But whatever the relationship, we cannot afford to spend too much time with low-flying small-thinking people. There may even be people that we love, but we still don't spend a great quantity of time with them. We all have thirty-minute people, fifteen-minute people, five-minute people, one-minute people, ten-second, five–second or even one-second people in our lives. After we are with these people for a certain number of minutes or seconds, they begin to drain us of energy. So the best approach with these folks is to know how to get away from them before the energy draining starts! We can very politely excuse ourselves from their presence, and they probably won't even know that we are "making a run" for a more healthy, uplifting environment!

In our business dealings it is the same way. Even though we may have wanted to do a certain deal, it is also best in business dealings to know where the fire exit is if things start to get weird and we start to sense that the people with whom we are dealing are not on the level. It is very handy to have previously noted exactly where the exit is so that you can make a quick escape if needed!

I am being a little "tongue in cheek" here about this,

but the serious truth is that most of the deals we got ourselves into when we felt the people were not honorable or
purpose-driven usually ended up being deals that have
gone bad. Very often we lose time and money, and possibly
our reputation is also tarnished in the process. Sometimes
the reason people will invest time, energy, and money to
go through with deals with questionable people may be
because they think they need that specific person to be successful, not realizing that a more solid, on-purpose person
may be just around the corner.

People make many commitments personally and professionally that they regret, from coaching the little league
team to doing a business deal, and they end up losing precious time, energy, and resources. In hindsight, they find
themselves wishing they had not given in to the guilt trip
and manipulation used by others to get them tied up in the
first place. It is amazing how much pain, loss, and disap-
pointment we can avoid if we are no longer controlled by
the opinions of others.

The only opinions that really matter

To be a skilled "ice breaker", it is helpful to have a good
support group. The only opinions we should be concerned
about are those of people we know to be principled, truth-
based purpose-driven people. It is very valuable to know
what our mentor thinks about us or what others think
about us who have the same kind of vision that we have.
Receiving input and feedback from those who are connected to us at a heart level is of great value. If we know
that their hearts are pure and free from selfish agendas,
then what they think should mean a lot to us because we
know that they are sincere and have our best interests in
mind. It is even more powerful when we have a true heartfelt nourishing relationship with the people we are working together with to go to the next higher level. There is

great power in agreement with the synergized unity of our success being connected to their success and their success being connected to ours. The small inner circle of people you are truly connected with on a heart level are the only people that it is best for you to be accountable to.

Accountability to our mentor and to a small group of like-minded creative people is not only good, it is essential for our maximum spiritual, mental, emotional, and business development. A Centurion, (an officer who was leader over 100 other soldiers in the Roman army) came to Jesus asking Jesus to heal his servant, and Jesus actually "marveled" at the faith of this man. The Centurion had a simple but very profound revelation. He knew that, as an officer in the Roman army, he had great authority, but he also knew that he only had this authority because he was "under the authority" of the entire Roman government. He also recognized that because Jesus was under the authority of his Father God Almighty, Jesus had authority to "speak the word only and my servant will be healed".

The truth-based-principle that is illustrated here is simply "to have true authority" we must first be "under authority." Any person who says, "I don't need a mentor, I can make it on my own" is a person who is not only fooling himself or herself but is also working in contradiction to this truth-based-foundational principle. We all need people we can confide in and trust to the fullest extent. There is a great difference between having people in our lives who like us and people who truly love us enough to tell us the truth in every situation. It may temporarily feel good to have "yes people" in our lives who tell us what we want to hear rather than what we need to hear. But in the long run the greatest value is to have a mentor who "loves us" more than "likes us". The people we are vulnerable to must be those who it is safe for us to be under their authority. These people may be few in number, but they are precious, and in some ways our connection with them is usually just as valuable to them as it is to us.

Learn how to overcome rejection by watching your mentor

I hope you have a strong mentor that you can look to, learn from, and duplicate in many ways. One very valuable lesson to learn from your mentor is how she or he handles rejection. Notice your mentor's body language when someone is rejecting his or her ideas. Does her or his voice volume go up or down? Does he or she begin to talk slower or faster after the apposing party has rejected her or his ideas or perhaps even insulted your mentor on some level? You will learn volumes by watching closely and taking mental notes. It may even be good to write down a note or two while you are experiencing this first-hand education in skilled human interaction. Often more is caught in the presence of your mentor, even beyond that which was deliberately taught.

I remember hearing a certain man talk of his great accomplishments, and then he made a strong point about how others could accomplish exactly what he did if they would just follow his simple instructions. After his explanation of the amazing things he had accomplished, he could tell by the look on their faces that the people listening were blown away by his story of success. He had seen that look before and knew those people were seeing him as one who had been bestowed with a lucky break that would probably not occur for them. This had caused the listeners to be detached from the fact that these accomplishments were also possible for them. Even though their reaction was for the most part positive, their extreme astonishment had caused a barrier between him and them, and he now found himself somewhat alienated from his listeners because they had mentally put him up on a pedestal.

As he made this observation, I noticed that he made an immediate adjustment to help the listeners make a shift in their perception. Once he felt the separation, he quickly followed with this statement. "I don't say all of this to impress you. I say this to <u>impress upon you</u> that if you follow the same steps that I have practiced, then you can accomplish what I have and maybe even something greater." Then he continued his presentation. By making that one statement, he took the spotlight off of himself and turned the light on to the success principles and laws that he had been practicing, therefore making the principles the star attraction!

The key thing to remember here is to not fall into the trap of seeing yourself through the eyes of other people. It is important that we do not become too impressed by others when they are impressed by us. It can be easy to be swept away by flattery or by disapproval. **We must stay aware that flattery and disapproval can, at times, be imposters.** It is not uncommon for people to like us one moment and then, without any obvious reason, show disapproval towards us the next. If we get swept away with either flattery or disapproval, we are rendered helpless to stay grounded on truth-based success principles because we have given more importance to people's opinions than to principle.

Most people usually see a distorted picture of us and themselves in context with any given conversation or interaction we have with them. As I have noted previously, in many cases people are so busy creating in their minds the next thing they want to say that they are distracted from truly listening to the person talking with them.

If you or I become preoccupied with the desire to impress the other person with our next brilliant comment, our listening ability is hindered and we may miss the major points the other person is saying to us through words, body language, and charisma. Often what a person is saying in words is the least important message. **In many cases the words people speak are a replacement for what they do not want to reveal to us.**

For example, a person usually would not want to come right out and say, "I feel that I am too insecure to believe I could be financially successful." Instead, they might say, "I cannot join you in your business opportunity because I am already too busy and I don't have time to do any more than what I am already doing." **When people make excuses for not being successful, they are often simply trying to avoid failure.** As strange as it may seem, it is very common for people to think that if they never try anything new, then they don't have to worry about failing!

To be an expert "icebreaker" requires focus and concentration in order to locate the areas that are unfulfilled in the lives of the people we are communicating with. If we can locate the areas of life that they feel they are lacking in, we will better be able to show them how the opportunity, vision, or idea we are presenting will be able to provide them with a more fulfilling life experience. A great "icebreaker" not only needs to discern the needs that a person has, but while melting and breaking the ice he or she also have to be able to fully listen and focus on what lies behind the words that a person is speaking. It requires our complete attention to pick up the hidden, insecurities, fears, strengths, potentials, etc., that often are revealed only in the more subtle nuances of a conversation.

Discerning exactly what other people's weaknesses are is the first step in our being able to help them to move beyond those weaknesses, to get unstuck, and to be released to go to a higher level.

If we will simply just be ourselves and the best person we can be, it will be easier to avoid being preoccupied with a need for their approval and to give our full attention to their needs. When their needs are met, our needs will be met in return. Yes, it is true and we need to remind ourselves of these truths constantly, "If you can help enough people get what they want, then you will inevitably end up getting what you want." And, "If you help enough other people get to their next higher level, then you will automatically end up on your next level." This is a law that will not fail: **"Give and you shall receive."**

As you observe a successful mentor, you will pick up useful tips and strategies that will increase your wealth of people skills. This will be of greater worth than a sack of gold or a box of diamonds!

I learned a very valuable lesson from a very successful person years ago: "Always make the vision or the opportunity the star." People can relate to a vision or an opportunity as the "star" better than they can relate to you as the "star."

Once I heard this man tell of his discovery that the *setting* of a meeting made all the difference in the number of recruits he was able to obtain.

He began by inviting people onto his $10,000,000 yacht. He thought they would be impressed that his business opportunity had provided this luxury for him, and thereby they would be convinced that this same business could provide similar luxuries for them. What he found was just the opposite. Bringing people onto his yacht actually served as a barrier for them to grasp the fact that his opportunity would work for them. It was too much of a stretch for them to believe for a $10,000,000 yacht. Their real needs were to believe they could pay off credit card debt or maybe take a nice vacation to Disney World. So this man switched his strategy and started showing people his opportunity either at their own kitchen table or at a casual restaurant. Sometimes he scribbled the numbers and details of the opportunity on a napkin or on a placemat at a restaurant. When he made this change in venue and approach, the number of people he recruited went up 90%! Sometimes it is only by trial and error that we discover the most effective way to help people become more open and receptive.

Yes, breaking the ice will necessitate that we put ourselves in the other person's shoes long enough to be able to make a solid connection. Being a good or even a great ice breaker has a lot to do with breaking through the hidden barriers that people have built up to protect themselves from being used or manipulated. Breaking the ice when we are first proposing a new idea to a person is also a matter of operating with compassion for the human condition, which is widespread in the world we are living in. For the most part there are more insecure people than there are confident people on this planet, and there are more people who are trying to hide behind a façade than there are people who are open and transparent. Understanding that most people will need our reassurance and our positive validation will help us to be more aware of their true heartfelt needs. As we concentrate on staying aware of their needs, this will help us to make a genuine connection with them, break through the veneer of their outer shell, and get to the heart of who they really are.

Chapter

3

Eliminate the "Fear of People"

Let me ask you a question. What if you could totally eliminate and completely lose one thing, this thing called "the fear of people"? What difference would this make in your ability to promote and enroll other people into your vision, mission, or business?

Of course, it is not the physical human beings we are dealing with that we fear. What we usually fear is the possibility that they will reject us. There are exceptions to this rule, of course, as in a situation when someone may be angry with us to the point of physically threatening us. In this case a certain type of fear is actually a form of wisdom and can help us produce the much needed adrenalin that will enable us to do whatever is necessary to get away from that person unharmed. But in most cases we don't actually fear the person as much as we fear that his or her opinion of us will be negative.

If I could guarantee that the next 100 people you called on the phone or you met with in person would be overjoyed to support you in whatever idea, vision, mission, or business that you proposed to them, how fast would you start dialing the phone to make your initial contacts with those next 100 people? What if I could guarantee that the next 100 people you contacted would say, "I am so glad that you contacted me. In fact I have been hoping that you would call me to give me a chance to work with you, and I am so excited about your ideas. I would be honored to have the opportunity to join you in the vision that you are working to make a reality. I can't wait to get started. Just let me know where to be and when to be there, and I'm with you 100%"? If you could be guaranteed this response, would you have any fear of picking up the phone to call a person that you consider the smartest, sharpest, most influential person you know?

Now, of course I cannot guarantee that this will happen; in fact, I can guarantee that a lot of people will not respond positively when you first contact them with any new idea. But what this "next 100 people" illustration very clearly shows is that if we can stay free from the fear of how people are going to react to us, then we will become fearless in promoting our vision and ideas. If we can stay mentally and emotionally detached from whatever that other person's initial reaction will be, we will be able to successfully remove the fear of people at the same moment that we successfully remove the need for them to approve of us and our ideas.

It is a fact that most people have no initial truth-based reason for rejecting us! In fact, they are often worrying about what our opinion is of them! So their defense mechanism kicks in, and they go on "automatic survival mode" to preserve their perceived image at any cost.

What you know determines who will want to know you

Let's go a little deeper with this point. Who you know is important. There is a great advantage in knowing and being accepted by the right people. But this is secondary to "what you know". The spiritual foundational principle "And you will know the truth, and the truth will make you free" is a law that works in forward motion or in reverse. Whether we know the truth or believe a lie will determine whether people sense an attractive charisma or a repelling charisma when they encounter us.

Yes, it is still true, and it will always be true that "As a man or a woman thinketh, so they will be," and "We are transformed by the renewing of our mind."

The simple fact is that if we are not on a solid foundation of truth-based thoughts about ourselves, our purpose, and our true value, ultimately we will be afraid of being rejected by other people. And if we are afraid of being rejected by other human beings, this "fear of rejection" will cause us to exude an "insecure charisma" that will make people want to get away from us as fast as they can. Therefore, "As we thought it to be, so it was for us," and sure enough, every time it will happen just exactly as we truly believe that it will.

Eliminating the "fear of people" is a vital step that is necessary in order for us to go to the next higher level in life, in business, in relationships, and in every other area of life. The "fear of people" is based on an incorrect perception of ourselves and an incorrect perception of others. To overcome this we must see ourselves and other people truthfully and accurately.

Our ability to be persistent and unstoppable is, to a great extent, determined by our perception. Why do some people, who seem to have fewer advantages and less going for them, keep going and win the big victories and successes in life, while other people, who seem to have all the advantages and appear to have everything going for them, give up and quit on their dreams and settle for a lower level? It is because one person had a perception that his or her purpose in life is to go to higher and higher levels of freedom and blessing, and the other person perceived himself or herself to not be capable or worthy of anything better in life.

It's not always the best looking, the smartest, or the person with the best education who gets ahead in life. It is the one with the right perception, the right belief system, and the right kind of charisma!

When we present an idea, business opportunity, or any kind of vision or plan to other people, we obviously want them to say, "Yes, I will join and support you." We want them to say, "That is a great idea...I want to get started on this project with you right now. How do we make this happen as fast as possible?"

However, if you have worked with people for very long at all, you know as well as I do that this is not the typical response. What is most important at that moment in time is not that they are offering resistance or they seem to be rejecting us. What is most important is that we know how to control our perception of what is really going on in the interaction between us.

All procrastination, fear, insecurity, etc. is a result of a truth deficiency in our thoughts. Just as a vitamin deficiency weakens our physical bodies, a truth deficiency will weaken our faith and our perception.

A distorted perception usually causes procrastination on our part and is evidenced in our avoiding the task of making phone calls or meeting with people. Remember this: "A truth-based perception produces unstoppable persistence."

Inspect their motives and their motivations

What really motivates them? If you do research and ask questions on the front end of the conversation, it will many times pay off "big time" on the back end. What are the motives that drive them? **Finding out what you think about them is more important than what they think about you**

If you concentrate on discovering their motives and motivations, you will not only often find out *what they want most in life,* but you will also find out more importantly *why they want it.* To put our full concentration on the other person, we must take the focus of our concentration off of ourselves. As long as we are wrapped up in the emotional quagmire of worrying about what they are thinking about us, we become the "needy" one and are open to being manipulated by them!

The fact is, *you can't concentrate on them and yourself at the same time.* In fact, your ability to let other people know that you are really interested in them and their needs will ultimately determine how much they will want to open up to you and reveal more of their true selves. The principle to remember here: "People don't care how much you know until they know how much you care."

Monitor other people's emotional state

Any time you can make people feel better about themselves or better about their life in general, you will have a greater advantage in communicating and working with them.

Many people need some emotional support in order for them to believe that they can succeed. There are some exceptions to this rule. Once in a while you or I will find a person who is already in a place in her or his mind and heart that enables them to have the confidence to take on big challenges and believe that they have "what it takes" to make it happen. But this type of person is very rare.

At the very first, most people do not agree to join with us in a pursuit because they really believe they will be successful or believe that the opportunity we are offering to them will actually work for them personally. So if most people don't have the confidence to be certain they are going to succeed, what is the main reason why many of them say yes and decide to join us? It is simply because <u>they liked the way it felt to be with us!</u>

It is important that we repeat and reinforce this principle every day. **"The main reason why most people first decide to say yes and join us in any pursuit is because we helped them to feel good about themselves when they were in our presence."**

For people to feel good when they are in our presence, we must be continually conscious that we are meeting the emotional needs of the person that we are talking with. In order to be able to do this, we must first check ourselves to make sure that we are not feeling "needy" in our present emotional state. If people observe that we need their approval, they will feel unsure and doubtful about us.

As we maintain a strong awareness of the truth of "who we really are," we are free to fully focus on the emotional needs of others. Do they need acceptance? Do they need to feel safe? Do they need approval? Do they need to know that they have what it takes to make it happen? Do they need to ask more questions? Do they need to feel more important? If you can help them to eliminate their emotional deficiencies they are much more likely to respond well to you and much less likely to reject you and your ideas.

If you are on a strong enough foundation of truth that you don't need the instant gratification of other people's emotional support, then you are free to emotionally support them and you will exude a charisma that gives them hope and confidence.

Monitoring the other individual's emotional state gives us the unique ability to keep our interaction with him or her on track and helps us to avoid meaningless chatter. We are at all times in control and have our first priority set as that of guiding the conversation in a direction that is best and most beneficial for us and for the other person.

You don't really need any one person or any one business deal

There will be another person or another deal that will come along in the next minute, day, or week.

Make up your mind beforehand that you don't really need that person or that deal and that you could walk away without their approval and still be just as strong and secure as you were before you talked with them. The point here is not that you or I should ever enter into a proposal of our ideas, vision, mission or opportunity to another person with an "I don't care" attitude. No, that is definitely not what I am suggesting. In fact we should go into every interaction visualizing a positive outcome. But since, to a certain degree the final outcome is going to be out of our control, we must also make it ok for there to be a less than 100% positive response from the other person. A good thing to remember is that we are not just looking for everyone and anyone to join us, we are looking for the people that we are purposed and predestined to work with. *We are sorting through people to find the ones that we are meant to be with.*

We do need people, and we do need business deals to turn out well in order to be successful, but we don't need any one specific person, and we don't need any one specific business deal. Any time when we are talking or negotiating with someone and begin to feel that we absolutely must have them or must have that specific business deal, we are setting ourselves up to be manipulated and rejected, because the other person can feel that we are out of balance and are coming from a place of insecurity.

One great way to avoid becoming discouraged is to remember this law: **"You must talk to the many to find the few."** If you obey this law, you can be assured that, "your own" will come to you. "Your own" means "the people whom you were destined to be with from before the beginning of time." You were meant to be with them, and they were meant to be with you, even before either of you were formed in your mother's womb. Destiny is a wonderful thing!

Act like you belong there!

We are all sales people. Even if you have never actually sold a product or service, you most likely are still involved in one type of selling or another every day of your life. You could be trying to sell your children on keeping their bedroom clean, negotiating to get a better price for a car, telling a friend about a restaurant you like, or explaining about something else you would like another person to buy into. Whether we are involved in selling as a profession or just in everyday life, it is one of the greatest opportunities that we will ever have for personal growth and increased self esteem.

Years ago from age twenty-two to twenty-six; I did some sales work that taught me many lessons that have been very valuable to me in all the years that have followed. I had my first experience in door-to-door sales, selling fire extinguishers to businesses. Next, I went on to sell advertising space in a magazine, and again this was door-to-door sales to businesses. Later, I was promoted to sales manager for that magazine and learned what it was like to have to find creative ways to keep the representatives in my sales force inspired and motivated on a daily basis. Along with the sales people that I would send out on the streets to sell magazine ads to businesses, we also started a telemarketing department, with twenty people in a room making phone calls to every business in the yellow page section of the local phone book.

Any type of sales provides a great growth experience because it forces us to face and overcome a lot of the fears, preconceived limitations, and insecurities that will continue to plague many people who have never had a big enough reason to grow out of the little box in which they live.

I remember one day when my mentor in the fire extinguisher business taught me a very important lesson. I had been going from door to door to businesses asking them if I could inspect their fire extinguishers to make sure that they were all in working order. If a fire extinguisher had lost pressure and the gauge read "empty," I would take it back to the shop so that it could be recharged. Also, if the company did not have enough fire extinguishers for the square footage of their buildings, I would sell them more fire extinguishers so that they would be fully protected with coverage in case of fire. There are different kinds of fire extinguishers for different work environments. If a room had a lot of computers in it, the type of fire extinguisher that I would install was one containing a substance that would not harm electrical equipment when it was discharged. If it was the kitchen area of a restaurant, then I would install a fire extinguisher containing an agent that would put out a grease fire. There were many other different types of units for various other business environments.

When I walked into a business the first few days I was in this sales position, I would ask if they had their fire extinguishers inspected within that past six months and if not, would they allow me to do an inspection? The person who I usually dealt with was the front desk secretary or maybe a manger. Very often that person would not know anything about their fire safety inspections and would go check their files to find out the answer to my question. Quite frequently, even if they had not had an inspection for several years, they would still not let me inspect their facility because they would find recorded in their files that a different fire protection company had done their last inspection, and they didn't know if they should switch companies.

I let the owner of the fire extinguisher company I was working for know about this resistance I was experiencing, and I also told him that it was hard to get these businesses to let me in to do the inspections. His response shocked me! He said, "Larry, don't ask them if you can inspect their fire extinguishers. It doesn't really matter to them who does the inspection. If you don't raise the question, they won't have to answer it. **You just need to act like you belong there!!** When you walk into a business, just walk up to the person at the front desk, show them our company business card, and say, "I'm here to inspect your fire extinguishers. I will start my inspection here in the office, and then I will need access to all of the other areas of your facility."

It was amazing to see what happened the next day when I used this new approach. I got into every business that I went to, sold a bunch of new fire extinguishers, and took a truckload of extinguishers back to the shop to be recharged. Needless to say, this really looked good when I received my commission check that week.

"You just need to act like you belong there." This is great advice for anyone. No matter where you are or who you are talking to, just **act like you belong there. Walk in like you belong there, talk like you belong there, and you** will find that most of the time, people will just assume that you do belong there. They will respect you as a person of importance, and they will see you as a person they need listen to!!

You are choosing who you do and don't want to work with

Here are some good questions to ask yourself when you are meeting someone for the first time. "Is this person going to be a nourishing influence or a toxic influence in my life or business?" Is this person someone I would want to spend a lot of time with? Is this person someone I would feel comfortable to allow to meet and spend time with my family?

Don't get tied up in "energy draining" relationships with people

We need to qualify every individual to see if they are the kind of person we want to be with and or work with. Your first priority is not to see if they want to be with you or work with you. You are the interviewer – that person is an applicant for a position with you in your life or your business!

Silence is just as important as talking

Let the other person talk. Many times when you have the greatest urge to talk, that is the exact time when you need to be silent and not say a word. It is common for us to not hear what the other person is saying, because while he or she is talking to us, we are more focused on reinforcing our point of view.

Resist the temptation to let your mind race ahead to what you hope will be the final outcome, even if it means you will have to pause for a second or two before responding to that individual. You will find that just a pause of one or two seconds can give you the time needed to make your response much more meaningful.

Another valuable point, in relation to the dynamics of conversations and negotiations, is that the exact time when we feel like raising our voice to emphasize a point, that is often the time when we need to lower our voice in order to make a point more impacting. Lowering our voice forces the other person to pay careful attention to what we are saying and will often set her at ease instead of putting her on the defensive. It is important that you always keep the other person leaning forward into your space. DO NOT lean forward into the other person's space. If you lean forward into another person's space, he or she may feel imposed upon. If you keep them leaning into your space, then you've got their full attention, and they feel in control, even through you are the one who is actually steering the conversation.

The more that we develop a strong sense of purpose and an accurate picture of who we have been created to be on the inside, the less we will fear other peoples reactions to us. You have gifts, talents, abilities and a vision that some people will greatly appreciate while other people won't be able to understand your uniqueness, let alone appreciate you or your vision for the future. Fearing the reactions of other people is a meaningless waste of time. But to stay centered enough to keep ourselves spiritually, mentally and emotionally strong enough to be able to eliminate the fear of people, we will need to be constantly reading the right books, listening to positive teaching tapes and CDs, listening to uplifting music, receiving input from our mentor and whatever else is necessary to keep our self image, our thoughts and our sense of worthiness on a high enough level. If you had twenty-four hours left to live, who would you choose to spend that time with? You would spend that time with those who love and appreciate you the most. Well, every twenty-four hours is a gift to be counted precious. We can give many people the opportunity to share the precious moments that we have to live. Some of these people will become life long loving friends and some of them will just be a passing encounter, but as long as we know that we are endeavoring to be the best that we can be we can let their reactions belong to them. Whether positive or negative they are the author of their thoughts and we are the author of our thoughts. I think that the children's song says it best "Accentuate the positive, eliminate the negative and don't mess around with Mr. in between"!

Chapter

4

Use the Layering Approach

During a recent trip to Australia I was having dinner seated next to a married couple who are leaders in the business group which brought me to Sydney to speak at their conference. We were talking about how we were all working on developing better eating habits and choosing foods with less fat, sugar or salt and eating more vegetables and meats that were baked, steamed, or broiled rather than fried. Sometime during that conversation this couple explained with great enthusiasm that they had rediscovered how much better poached eggs taste when they took the time to put water in a pan, allow the water to start to boil, and then crack the eggs and drop the yoke and white of the egg into the water to cook for a short time. They said that for years during their daily breakfasts together they had been poaching their eggs in a plastic egg poacher that they put in the microwave oven, and one day they just decided to try cooking the eggs the old fashioned way. They said, "Wow, the eggs taste so much better when we take that little extra time to cook them in boiling water on the stove!"

With the invention of microwave ovens, jet travel, instant mashed potatoes, computers, and countless other ways to speed up the process of completing different tasks, we have all grown accustomed to getting many things done in just a matter of minutes or even seconds. But there are some things that cannot be rushed without compromising the integrity of the final outcome. Very often this "get it done quickly" mentality has also greatly influenced how we interact and build relationships with people. In this fast-paced world we can tend to be in too much of a hurry when first proposing an idea, vision, or opportunity to a prospect. At times it is just a simple matter of wanting things to happen faster than the best natural methods of operation will allow, but sometimes there are other underlying reasons why a person will try to build rapport and seal the deal too speedily. For instance, if we have any "fear of people" still influencing us, or if we struggle with feelings of unworthiness, insecurity, or high levels of negative self-talk, we may actually self-sabotage a conversation. By rushing to tell the whole story and overloading the prospect with too many details in the first presentation, a person who fears failure may have already supposed that he would most likely be rejected. Therefore this person could unconsciously figure that he may as well get it over with quickly and make the impending rejection as short-lived and painless as possible.

Whatever the reason is that we may feel the need to rush and try to get to the bottom line too quickly, at that moment we need to take a deep breath and realize that the relationship we are building with another person is more important than the bottom line we are working towards. Even if the person to whom we are proposing our vision, mission, or opportunity responds in the affirmative during our first conversation, if we have not established a mutual respect and a real connection with that individual, there is a high probability that the next time we meet, he or she may have lost interest or had a change of mind.

Some negotiations can be done quickly—like negotiating for a better seat on an airplane or getting a better price on a floor display model of an appliance at a store. But in these instances there is no real need to build a life-long relationship with the person we are dealing with.

The bigger the commitment that you are asking the other person to make, the more it may be necessary to break up what you are sharing into bite-sized pieces and let that person digest one portion at a time.

The fact is, if the vision we are proposing to people has a fairly large or even a huge scope to it, the best approach is usually to not try to get a 100% commitment from people the first time we share our vision with them.

I will be the first to admit that many of the greatest successes I have experienced often came about as a result of much persistence on my part. In fact, as I have studied the lives of very successful people, I have found that they were not always those who had the highest IQ or the most impressive education or family heritage. But in the majority of successful individuals I've studied, there was a quality of "refusing to quit" even when the odds seemed to be stacked against them, with one road block after another presenting itself. But in the face of even seemingly insurmountable odds they forged ahead until they split the roadblocks in half and kept on truckin'!

My next statement may seem strange to some readers, but others will understand and relate completely to what I am about to say. **I have come to regard rejection as an old friend that I will most likely encounter several times and sometimes many times along the road that leads to each new higher level in my life. I believe that to try to avoid rejection is very close to trying to avoid success. They always come together. Rejection can be the one who makes you smarter, kinder, more humble, and a better communicator. Use it, learn from it, and then rise above**

it. You can either turn rejection into gold or let it rust you out and corrode your mind and emotions. It all depends on how you deal with it.

Since it is true that during their first exposure, some people are not going to fully accept and support us and our ideas, vision, mission, or business opportunity, it makes sense to have a long-term strategy planned out ahead of time.

We need to give most people several, sometimes many, small doses or "layers" of whatever we are proposing to them. It would be nice if there was a magic wand we could wave to make this work differently, but there really is no viable substitute for good, old fashioned relationship-building skills. As in many areas of life, trying to take a shortcut will usually greatly decrease the quality of the outcome in relation to building rapport with people.

About thirty years ago I painted houses for a living. I did this for only a short time because I really did not enjoy having the smell of paint fumes up my nose all day long. But I was in the house-painting business long enough to learn a few truth-based foundational principles about house painting.

First of all, if the old paint on the house was peeling, cracked, and chipped, then I would have to scrape and sand that old stuff off before I could apply a fresh coat of paint.

Second, to do a proper job, I would have to apply some kind of crack filler to all of the cracked surfaces that could not be removed during the scraping and sanding process.

The third fact I learned is that you can't apply water-based paint directly onto a surface that was formerly painted with oil-based paint, because "water and oil don't mix," and the water-based or latex paint will just peel off when it dries.

Fourth, if you want to cover an oil-based painted surface with water-based paint, you would have to apply some kind of really nasty smelling primer first., Sometimes it would take two or more layers of this primer before the porous wood would stop soaking it up and there would be a solid surface to work with.

Fifth, once the surface was prepared properly, at least two coats of paint were usually necessary to do a good quality job of painting the exterior of a house. On occasion three coats were necessary if the wood had weathered badly or was very porous. So I had to keep putting on another layer of paint until the entire surface had an even and consistent look to it.

Sixth, when using oil-based paint or even water-based paint, if I tried to apply one really heavy coat onto the surface instead of taking the time to apply two or three lighter coats, the result was a total painting disaster. I remember trying to take this shortcut at the beginning of my very short painting career. I thought that if I was very careful and the humidity was not very high that day, the paint would dry quickly... I figured that I could get the job done in half the time and I would make twice as much money per hour because I would only have to work half the hours and still be paid the same amount of money for the total job.

I very soon found out that operating according to the "one heavy coat instead of two or three lighter coats" theory was in total opposition to the laws that apply to successful house painting. Even if the paint seemed to go on okay at first, over a period of time the paint would begin to drip, and the whole side of the house would look horrible...

One experience of having to scrape off that gooey, sticky fresh paint and having to, re-sand, and re-paint the whole side of a house was all it took. I learned my lesson well and never tried to shortcut the process again. In fact, from that point on I probably applied even thinner layers and more coats than I actually had to just to make sure that the "shortcut" disaster of "laying it on too thick" would never happen again.

Proposing a new idea, vision, mission, or business opportunity to a person works similarly in principle to painting a house. With most people you will have to be patient until they eventually let down their defenses and remove the old layers and the barriers of their self-protective mechanisms.

Next, you may have to apply a few layers of primer or encouraging words to fill in the cracks in their self image in order to help them feel better about themselves and let them know they are safe and you are not trying to misuse or manipulate them.

Then after one, two, three, or even more encounters with them, they may finally let you apply the first real layer of what your idea, vision, or opportunity is really about. You may have been trying to apply the first layer during the first time you talked with them, but even with the best communicators their first conversation is often just a warm-up step toward helping the other person to open up enough to fully hear what they are saying.

When they feel better about themselves they will feel better about you too!

It is helpful to be aware that the first time we talk with an individual, it is not uncommon to find that he or she has a less than strong self-image., It is sad to say, but there are a fairly large number of people wandering the planet with a less than zero self-esteem level.. Many people's self image is so damaged that by the time you or I get to them to propose any new idea that will help them get to the next higher level personally or professionally, they really cannot buy the fact that they could become a real success at much of anything.

But if we are willing to apply one thin layer after another, it can be absolutely amazing to see the change that can occur in the people who seemed totally shut down and even negative the first time we talked with them. They can actually transform into a completely different positive person after we have patiently applied several light layers of our charisma, vision, and inspiration.

Very much like a person's physical body will become weak or even sick if not nourished properly, a person's self-esteem also needs to be nourished. If we have a vitamin deficiency it can take weeks or months of taking vitamins to get our levels up where they should be. There is not usually a "one dose cure" to make up for a deficiency in our physical, mental, or emotional state.

If we take a few vitamins each day, our health condition most likely will improve. If we swallow the whole bottle of vitamins in one day, it will make us sick to our stomachs, and we might even get so sick that we have to vomit or have our stomachs pumped out.

By giving people small regular doses of what we have to share, we can build up their expectation level one layer at a time until finally one day we notice that something is different. They hit critical mass, and they are "locked and loaded" and ready to go. Some folks will sign on the dotted line and tell you that they are with you 100%, but the way you will know if they are really with you and your vision is if they take action on the steps you are teaching them to take. With some of those people, when they were at the beginning of the layering process, you may have been wondering if you were wasting your time working with them. Yet amazingly enough, some of these very people will surprise you and become your greatest supporters.

Often people are incapable of feeling good about you or the possibilities that you are sharing with them until you first help them feel better about themselves. As you help people to feel better about themselves, it is quite natural for many of them to start feeling better about you too!

While you are layering don't be too accessible

When we are meeting with people over and over with the purpose of applying another light layer, it is a good idea, in most cases, to make ourselves a bit scarce in between encounters. Until a person has made a full commitment that she or he is with us 100% and is going to take full action on the steps of success that we are teaching, he or she should only have limited access to us.

Now of course there are exceptions to this rule when it comes to family and close friends, but even in these cases it is often best for them to see that we don't have time to waste. Diamonds are considered to be of great value because they are rare, scarce, and hard to find, but when you pay the price to get in the presence of a great quality diamond...wow, do they sparkle. Be a diamond!

Keep them wanting more...

People love intrigue, especially in business and in romance. At the very beginning of a relationship, a little space and a little distance between encounters is generally a good thing.

If you are too accessible, too easy to reach on the phone,

and your schedule is so wide open that people can always call you or get together with you for a visit at a moments' notice, then they probably won't put a very high value on your time.

In many cases it is better for people to see that you are a person who has a full enough schedule that you are too busy to meet with them today but that you could fit them into your schedule to get together with them tomorrow or in a few days. At the beginning of a relationship even if you don't have much going on that day, you still don't want to appear too easy or too available.

People put a higher value on busy people and a lower value on people who do not consider time to be a precious thing. If you can keep other people fitting into your time frame and avoid always trying to fit into their time frame, in the long run their respect level for you will steadily increase.

The individual to whom we are proposing our ideas needs to know that the vision, purpose, idea, or opportunity that we are offering to them is so big that it could never be completely explained in one phone call or during one meeting. It is often best if we *very subtly* make them aware that it will take several meetings for us to be able to fully explain the potential of success in what we are sharing with them. We can also let them know that the reason we are willing to invest the time to share the total vision with them is because we believe that they could be very successful in the vision or opportunity that we are explaining to them.

If this is their perception, they will put a higher value on our time together and will be much less likely to take us for granted. Each time we meet, they should leave our presence with a feeling of wanting to hear more, learn more, and receive more from us.

How to communicate with strong, centered, "On Purpose" people

In some of the previous paragraphs I have talked about how to overcome rejection when communicating with the majority of people we will encounter as we walk, drive, or fly around the world. As we have cited earlier, the average person's self esteem is rather low, and she or he is possibly quite unclear about his or her purpose.

These people are "the masses" who very often drag themselves to a job they dislike each day and have settled for a lower level in life and may not even believe that a higher level is even available for them.

Now let's "shift gears" and talk about how to overcome or rise above perceived rejection as we are communicating with strong, centered, "On Purpose" people.

These are often people who are very busy with a productive mission-centered life. These people are very rare. They are the top 20% of the top 20%, which is the top 4% of the achievers in the world. They are the crème de le crème, the best of the best, the movers and shakers. These are those who are already making great things happen. Often they already have a degree of freedom that the average person only dreams of having.

When you communicate an idea, vision, mission, or opportunity in which you would like to enroll these people, your approach needs to be from a somewhat different perspective than when you propose an idea to the average person.

A layering approach is also often needed with these high performance people but for different reasons than we use it with the common thinking, average person.

To get the attention of purpose-driven people, you must

be able to quickly show them that whatever you are offering to them is of great value. And they must be able to quickly see enough value to convince them that they may be missing out on something big and therefore have no choice but to at least stop and "take a look." Piquing people's true interest is a major key to getting their full attention.

These "On Purpose" people usually are not easy to reach on the phone or to pin down for a meeting. You may have to go through a secretary, an assistant, or a series of voice mail systems to get through to them. These folks are focused on a certain way of thinking, which pretty much adds up to this question: "What will be the most productive way for me to invest my time today?" So somehow we must, very quickly and in the fewest words possible, prove to them that what we are offering is of great enough value for them to take a few of their precious moments to listen. You probably know exactly what I am talking about as I mention this type of person, because if you have read this far into this book, you may very well be this kind of person yourself. Through research it has been shown that the average person may read a whole romance novel or finish an action novel but will not finish reading a book or listening to a complete tape or CD series that will actually improve that individual's life!

After you have successfully piqued the interest of a purpose-driven, centered person, you may still need to apply many layers. But the layers must be brushed on with a more heightened sensitivity than you would need in your approach with an average achiever.

For the purpose-driven mover and shaker type people, the layers must be applied with pinpoint accuracy. They are already so busy that when you get them on the phone, you will often have to condense to sixty seconds or less the total thought you want to convey to them.

You have to be ready for the possibility that your conversation could be interrupted by a call for them on another line or by someone else in the room with them. Obviously you don't have to be quite as concerned with helping these people to build better self esteem because they usually already have a pretty strong sense of self worth, which they have derived from their many great accomplishments.

I must also mention here that an outwardly successful person is not always an inwardly successful person. It continually amazes me how some people react to outward success and wealth by becoming more humble and thankful, while other people react to the same kind of outward success by becoming pompous and arrogant.

So while we are talking about "strong people" with "good self esteem", we also must be aware that there are "outwardly strong people" who do not have "inner strength" and whose self image is distorted. Some of these folks have huge egos. I personally prefer working with people who have a foundation of humility in their spirit and their personality. But working with people who have "over-inflated egos" can sometimes become a positive experience if you can do something to readjust the atmosphere immediately surrounding your encounter with them.

In these cases I have found that one of the best ways to disarm them is to let them do most of the talking and then with a humble posture gently guide them in the direction you want them to go. I have found that if I can maintain humility in my charisma while dealing with this type of people, there are times when they will actually "drop their act" and get real with me!

This world is filled with people who have egos that are driven by insecurity. Some of these people want to be free from the insecure feelings that pervade their lives, and some do not want to be free. It does seem strange that a person would choose to not be free, but some folks are so blinded that their distorted view of the world and other people has caused them to see people as pawns to be manipulated for their benefit.

So before you invest too much time in this type of a person, it is best to evaluate whether it is going to be a wise investment of your time and energy. Often it is a good idea to avoid working with people who have over-inflated egos, because it may be very energy draining to be around them. Also, the time and energy that you may spend trying to tip-toe around this type of person could be more productively invested in someone who has a balanced and teachable attitude.

Having said that, I must also say that there are people who may seem to have a bit of an over-inflated ego at first, but over time they can still become good people to work with. The thing to look for in a person like this is whether they have a desire for personal growth. Even if they seem a little abrasive at first, if they are willing to grow, than I will gladly work to help them realize a positive change in their life. Properly channeled, they can change their abrasive outgoing energy to an outgoing energy that still has the positive power of their personality continuing to flow but without the irritating element.

Healthy self-esteem people

Once you have made the initial contact with a focused person with healthy self-esteem, even if you are able to pique their interest during the first phone call or in a face to face meeting, a lot of persistence may be needed on your part to create any kind of momentum.

Now, I don't mean to sound discouraging. I am just being truthful about the way it really is. There may be a few exceptions, but for the most part, just the initial challenge of getting in direct personal contact with these people will cause the average person to become discouraged enough to give up and move on to someone who is easier to get in contact with.

But if you "pay the price" to earn the respect and interest of an already focused, purpose-driven person, you will find that all of your persistent efforts and creativity will often be a very worthwhile investment. You can be paid back with so many blessings that you will have no regrets about the hours of creative thinking and countless phone calls you invested in this type of relationship.

Persistence pays off "big time"

Years ago, I remember hearing about an organization that produced conferences throughout the world. A fellow public speaker told me that it was not uncommon for this organization to have ten thousand or even twenty thousand people in attendance at a single event. I was somewhat familiar with this group of business people because I had spoken at several smaller satellite events for associates within this organization with crowds of five hundred to two thousand people.

In my heart, I felt very strongly that I was purposed to speak at their largest conferences. I was told by others in the speaking business that the people at the top of the decision-making process for these large conferences were almost impossible to get in touch with. But amazingly enough I ended up speaking with a top level officer of this organization on the phone one day. He called me because he had heard from someone that I had some information he needed. When I received his phone call, I was bewildered that of all the people he could have called, he called me. Then it hit me. I had been praying that this door would open for me to speak at these huge conferences, and this was the *open door* in answer to those prayers.

I have found that even when a door of opportunity may initially seem to swing wide-open; it may still take a lot of hard work and persistence to actually get through the doorway.

This is good because it causes a process of growth within us. If things come too easily, we tend to not really appreciate them. Often success that comes too easily can be harmful to us because our character may not have developed to be strong enough to keep us thinking right.

If our character has grown to a lower level than the level of our achievements, this "character shortage" can cause us to lose perspective, and we can run our train off the track.

Well, I had a few conversations with this top leader within this organization, but the only thing we talked about was what he wanted to talk about and the information and situation that he was hoping I could help him with.

During those first few phone calls, I never mentioned the fact that I wanted to speak at his conferences. I didn't really understand back then what was actually happening during those first few conversations, but now I see it very clearly. Those first few phone conversations were the first "light layers" that were building a connection and a trust level between this gentleman and me.

After I had supplied all of the information he needed, I finally brought up the subject. I asked, "How would I go about being considered to speak at your national conferences? I have spoken at some of the smaller meetings that your associates have held, and my message seems to be right on target for the people in your business." His response was, "Larry, do you have a tape recording of one of your presentations?" I said, "Yes, I do." He said, "Can you send me a copy of that tape?" I said "Absolutely, I'll get it in the mail to you today." I hung up the phone and got that tape in the mail.

For the next several months I called this man over and over again. He was on my prospect list as one of many people I was calling throughout each day to have similar conversations with. All of these contacts were with individuals I hoped would invite me to come and speak to their groups.

But when I would look at my daily call list, his name always stood out because of the sheer size of the events that he produced. Every time I would call him, I would think, "Maybe this is the day that he will say yes."

I was always positive and hopeful in my approach, but it seemed as though I was getting nowhere. I made over twenty phone calls to this man, and with each phone call I had to find another creative way to ask the same question-- "Did you get a chance to listen to my tape yet?" Each time he would politely tell me "No, I'm sorry; I haven't gotten a chance to listen to it yet." I would than ask, "When would be a good time for me to call you back?" He would tell me a variety of things from one phone call to the next, but since this man was always flying to different countries all around the world, one of the responses that I would often hear from him was, "Larry, I have to go out of the country, so can you give me a call in two weeks?" I would say, "Yes sir, I will call you in two weeks. Have a great trip!"

Two weeks later I would look at my list of people I needed to call that particular day and would see his name. As I dialed the number I knew that if I was fortunate, this would be one of those days when he was in the office. If he was not in the office, I would ask his assistant to tell him that I had called and to please give him a message that I would call back later.

Keeping the ball in your court

Here is a communication tip that I have found to be very valuable: *If you are calling someone who is very busy and has a very hectic schedule, it is sometimes best not to leave a message for them to call you back.*

Once you have developed a strong enough relationship with that individual, then you can leave your phone number and a message for them to call you back. But until you have developed a strong enough "what is in it for them" factor and until you have laid enough layers on that relationship, it is usually best never to "leave the ball in their court." If you leave a message for them to call you back and they don't return your call and three weeks go by...there can be a potentially awkward situation starting to brew.

If you call them again, they know that they didn't return your phone call, and they can feel embarrassed, or you can feel as though you are intruding, and the whole balance of communication can get totally out of sync.

So the best M.O. is to keep the ball in your court. If you never ask them to call you back, then you can continue to call them a hundred times, and as long as you can keep your charisma, your posture, and your attitude right...you will keep the door open for future communication.

Butterflies and mosquitoes are both bugs

There is a reason why people like to have butterflies flying around them but don't like mosquitoes. Many people stop contacting and calling a person to "lay the next layer" because they start to feel as if they are bugging the person.

It may be true that after five or ten phone calls or meetings with an individual whom you know has great potential; you may feel like you are starting to bug them. But if you need to bug someone in order to be able to "lay the next layer", then just make sure that you are a butterfly and not a mosquito. If you are pleasant and kind and enjoyable to talk with, they might even start to look forward to your next contact!!!

Being a bug starts to pay off

So I dialed the phone to make another contact with this gentleman, with the number of calls now stacking up well into the double digits. His assistant said those wonderful words, "Yes, he is in the office. Can I put you on hold for a minute?" After a minute or two he got on the line and said, "Hello, Larry." This time he didn't even wait for me to ask the question because by now he knew why I was calling. He said, "I am very sorry, but I still haven't had a chance to listen to your tape." I said, "I understand, and I know that you are a very busy man. I don't mean to bug you too much about this--" He interrupted me in mid-sentence and said, "Larry, yes you do mean to bug me, and you are going to keep on bugging me until I listen to that tape! I respect your persistence. I have your tape right here on my desk, and I am going to put it in my car tonight and listen to it while I drive home from the office." Then he added, "Larry, can you call me tomorrow? I promise I will have listened to your tape and will have an answer for you." I said, "Yes, I will be happy to call you tomorrow. Would it be better for me to call you in the morning or in the afternoon? ". He said, "Right after lunch would be great. At about 1:00 PM would work fine". I said, "Great, I will call you at 1:00 PM sharp!!"

Now if you had been with me each time I called and had a conversation with this fellow and you had been counting the number of conversations, you would have found that the number of "light layers" I had applied to this business relationship was up to twenty-one, and now I finally have a promise that he would listen to the tape.

I believe that you and I must have an unstoppable attitude if we are going to create a breakthrough in situations like this. If you really want something, you will just keep calling a person until they either say "Yes" or they ask you to stop calling them!!

The next day I made that twenty-second phone call, or we could say that I laid the twenty-second layer onto this business relationship. He answered the phone and said, "Larry, I listened to your tape. It was great. I have four dates for you to speak. It will be four consecutive Fridays--the first will have 16,000 people in the audience, the second will have 10,000 people, the third will have 13,000 people, and the fourth conference will have 6,000 people in the audience." I sent a speaking contract to him for those four dates, and he sent back to me the signed contract and a 50% deposit of my speaking fees to hold those dates on my calendar and also a check with payment for my airfare expense for those four dates.

After twenty-two layers, I now had a contract to speak to over 45,000 people live, face to face, over one month's period of time. Was that worth twenty-two layers and twenty-two phone calls? Yes, you better believe it was more than worth it. Not only did I speak to those 45,000 people live, but in addition to that, one of the recordings of those Friday live presentations was selected as the third of many of my audio tape/CD programs to be distributed as a "tape of the week," to hundreds of organizations and hundreds of thousands of people around the world!

What if I would have given up and stopped making those phone calls after about ten or twelve layers? Wouldn't that have been sad? Look at what I would have missed!

Now I must interject here again that this man was one of many, many people that I was calling each week, so if he had never said yes, I was still going to be okay, and my business would still grow. I was not desperate. If we allow ourselves to become desperate for any one deal or any one person, it will probably cause us to repel that person or that deal. It is important that we stay far away from being desperate. **One way to avoid becoming "desperate" is to always be actively pursuing and developing three times the amount of business that you would actually need to make it. If you keep making three times the amount of phone calls and keep three times the number of potential clients on the table at all times, then you have the relaxed feeling of knowing that even if two out of three somehow fall through the cracks and even if two out of three end up amounting to nothing, you will still be just fine.**

Relaxed Intensity

"Relaxed Intensity" is knowing that you don't have to hear people say "yes" in order for you to feel good about yourself. It's making sure that your self esteem is in no way connected to their opinion. By using the word "relaxed", I do not mean that you would appear dull or withdrawn in any way. In fact, you can still have all of the passion and enthusiasm and even have a strong sense of urgency. The main distinction here is that you always want to be attracting people with your passion and strong belief in the vision or possibility you are presenting without ever appearing anxious or needy. When we are attracting people with "relaxed intensity", we have our feet firmly established on a strong foundation of confidence and therefore have a strong sense of balance. But when we are leaning forward to try to get people, the very fact that we are leaning forward to try to get them to agree with us, causes us to be off balance and actually gives the other person the "upper hand" in steering the conversation.

Another key ingredient needed for you to create "relaxed intensity" is for you to take such massive action by way of the large number of phone calls that you make and many people that you share your vision with on a regular basis that you build up a great amount of momentum. **There is a big difference between people who try to build their success as though it were a "hobby" and people who build success as a result of becoming men or women who are "on a mission" to make their visions and dreams become manifested reality. When you have built up enough momentum, you can be sure that over time the numbers are always going to work out in your favor.**

"Relaxed intensity" is just the opposite of worrying and being nervous every day because everything hangs on whether two or three people are going to say "yes" or "no". "Relaxed intensity" is a "knowing" that you have "put enough out there" that the law of reciprocity will take good care of you. Simply stated: "As you give, so you shall receive". If you share your vision with a small number of people, you will probably experience a small amount of success. Share your vision, mission, ideas, or opportunity with massive amounts of people, and over time it will come back to you in the form of massive success.

It is absolutely amazing what has happened over the past sixteen years since I spoke to those 45,000 people in one month. When we pay the price for seeing a breakthrough take place in our life, often we reap compounding residual benefits for years to come. As I mentioned earlier, one of the things that had put me "in the loop" of this business network was my having spoken at some smaller events in this same area of business during the previous few years. The very first speaking engagement in this specific area of business was in 1989 during a period of time when I had seemed to have hit rock bottom in many areas of my life.

Our ultimate success <u>will not</u> be determined by how faith-filled, purpose-driven, and mission-focused we can stay on the easiest days, but rather, our ultimate success <u>will</u> to the greatest extent, be determined by how strong, faith-filled, purpose-driven, and mission-focused we can stay on what seems to be the hardest and most challenging days.

On the days when things seem to be flowing smoothly, it is not as hard to take the action necessary to keep the "layering approach" momentum going. But I have found it is often on the days when I really don't feel like making the phone calls or feel like going into action to meet with people that some of the greatest successes have occurred. If you are faithful to consistently keep applying layers on the easier days as well as the more challenging days, you will have many instances where you get to the end of the day and say to yourself, "I am so glad I did not give into the temptation to blow this day off. This has been one of the most productive days of my life!"

Chapter

5

Never quit – Never give up

The ability to stay purpose-driven during all of the different seasons of life is a major key to overcoming rejection and the manifestation of phenomenal breakthroughs that will occur down the road.

The words "Never Quit and Never Give Up" are miracle-working words, and I must admit--and I am sure that I am not alone when I say this--**"There have been times in my life when the main reason why I did not give up was simply because I did not believe in quitting!"** At times we may not have any tangible evidence that things are ever going to get better. During those times it is helpful for us to know that there are unavoidable seasons of life that everyone must go through, and it is our choice whether we simply go through those seasons or if we choose to *grow* through each season. There is the springtime, when you plow the field and plant the seeds; there is summertime when you water the plants that are growing and make sure that the weeds do not overtake your garden; there is the fall season when you harvest your crops and reap the benefits of your labor; and there is the winter season. Wintertime in northwestern Pennsylvania, where I was born and raised and now live, can be brutally cold with a lot of ice and snow. I remember very well many winter-like seasons of my life when I was working as hard as I could to get to the next higher level of my dream-purpose. At these times nothing seemed to be growing at the moment and even my greatest efforts and hardest work did not seem to be paying off. There were many times when the only thing that got me through another day was the fact that I had a rock solid belief that the season would eventually change. I believed that if I didn't give up, that even though I had hit bottom and I seemed to be in the middle of a "wintertime season." if I could hold on and hold the vision of the next higher level I was working toward, then sooner or later I would enter into a "springtime season" when I could rebuild and replant.

There have been many, many days in the past when that was all that I had to hang on to. During some seasons of life we have to simply lay it all on the line and bank on the belief that **if we can stay purpose-driven, keep our thoughts right, work as hard as we can, and be a blessing to as many people as we can be on a daily basis, then at some point the season will change, and we will always hit our critical mass. Reaching "critical mass" is a nuclear term for when the nucleus of an atom splits and energy is released and an explosive chain reaction occurs in the surrounding atoms. These surrounding atoms also release their energy which either produces usable nuclear power or a massive explosion. We also reach a type of "critical mass" when we have taken enough consistent productive action to cause a breakthrough to take place which propels us to our next higher level.** The wonderful thing I have found is that without exception **"refusing to quit" has eventually resulted in victory every time.**

At times we can be tempted to reject ourselves!

If you read my book *The Magic Is In The Extra Mile*, you may remember that I shared about the time in my life back in the years of 1989-1990 when I slept on the office floor for a period of almost seven months because I did not have enough money to live anywhere else.

I'm not going to tell the whole story here but just touch on a few parts from that period of my life to emphasize a very important point. I am also going to give you a new updated report on some amazing things that have happened since I wrote about this in my last book.

In your life and mine the story continues to unfold, and years down the road we can look back and see more clearly how worthwhile it was, and still is, to steadfastly hold the right vision, even in the toughest of times.

Often what seems to be a "breakdown" in our lives is really the process that we needed to go through to create a "breakthrough." I was very tempted to view sleeping on that office floor as a "breakdown." I remember lying on that floor, looking up at the bottom of my desk and wondering if I had lost my mind and made the biggest mistake of my life. Then I thought, "Well, at least I'm not alone!" because in the office right next to mine, my newly found mentor, motivational speaker Les Brown was also sleeping on the floor in his office. But than I thought, "Maybe we are both crazy!" Living in that office on the twenty-first floor of the Penobscot Building in downtown Detroit, Michigan was a real opportunity to reject myself as a total looser.

Before moving to Detroit, I lived in Pennsylvania, and I had been doing very little traveling for speaking engagements. Mostly I spoke only at meetings within a sixty- to ninety-mile radius of my local area, and I also hosted a weekly ABC affiliate TV program and a five-day-a-week radio program for a number of years.

The main reason I moved to Detroit was to work with Les so that I could fulfill the vision my mother had spoken to me thousands of times while I was growing up.

Every day my mother would say to me, "Larry, you are going to grow up, have a message burning on your heart, and you will speak to tens of thousands of people". I resisted and did not believe her words for the first seventeen years of my life, and I caused my mother and father many problems and disappointments during those years. In fact, until the age of seventeen, I looked and acted more like someone who would end up in prison rather than on a speaking platform. I finally had a major life change and accepted this vision and purpose for myself shortly after my seventeenth birthday.

I am so very grateful to my mother and father for not giving up on me or rejecting me. My mother was the one who would speak the word to me, and my father, though a "man of few words," was always a tower of strength and love. They both held that vision for me and believed in me when I didn't believe in myself. My mother was only here on earth for a short time after I had this change of life and purpose. In fact, the first time that I spoke publicly to a group of people, she was sitting in the front row listening to me and supporting me, and thirty days later she died and went home to be with the Lord. I don't know if she can see what has been happening in my life since then, but I would like to believe that from heaven she has been able to see how the vision that she held for me has become a manifested reality.

From the very beginning when I started to flow in my purpose, I knew that to fulfill this vision of "speaking to tens of thousands of people," there would come a time when I would begin to travel and speak nationally and internationally.

Though I did continue to speak to small groups of people while in my twenties and thirties and also began to reach many more people through television and radio, I still knew in my heart that the vision to "speak to tens of thousands of people", meant that I was purposed to share principles with people that would enrich their lives in a "live" face-to-face setting in meeting rooms, auditoriums, and coliseums around the world.

So when the opportunity to work with Les Brown opened up, I did not hesitate to take the leap of faith to start traveling and speaking on a national level. I stopped doing the weekly ABC affiliate TV program, and stopped doing the five-day a week radio programs, and moved to Detroit "on faith," believing that working with Les Brown, who was already speaking on the national level, would provide the mentorship needed for me to launch into speaking nationally as well. I am very grateful to Les for believing in me and helping me to get to the next higher level during those trying days that occurred more than sixteen years ago.

Previous to sleeping on the office floor, I had moved into the third bedroom of Les's house. Then after a series of unforeseen challenges we ended up living and sleeping in the office.

Just one day before finding out that we were going to need to live in the office for a while, my car was stolen in downtown Detroit, and my insurance coverage was not sufficient for me to immediately buy another car. So, my choices for transportation were to ask people for a ride, borrow someone's car, or ride on public transportation. During this time Les, his cousin, whose real name was Alexander, but we called him "Bou", and I would get up early every day and take turns going to shave and get cleaned up in the public restroom. Then I would go to my desk and make between sixty and one hundred phone calls per day to try to find groups who would contract me to come speak at their meetings.

For years previous to this point I had a great hunger

to assimilate positive truth-based thoughts from whatever source I could find. Thought-exchange and thought-replacement was a part of my daily routine, and I believed very strongly in the power of praying, of reading, and of listening to positive teaching tapes and CDs, as well as making sure that I was regularly listening to uplifting music. But at this specific time while living in that office, I read more books than I had ever read, listened to more teaching and inspirational tapes and CDs than I had ever previously listened to, and I prayed more than I had ever prayed before. I had to flood my mind and heart with truth-based success principles all day long, every day, to avoid becoming depressed and to stay positive and optimistic.

Things were very tough for over six months, and I could not pay many of my bills. During this time I was really tempted to "reject myself" and the vision for my higher level and purpose in life. I remember looking out that twenty-first floor, Penobscot office building window many times at two or three o'clock in the morning, and negative thoughts would just begin to roar through my mind. I would think, "Larry, you are a fool, you are crazy, you're never going to make it, and you are also a hypocrite and a fraud, because you are talking to groups of people about success while your life is going down the toilet". I would take the cushions off of the office waiting-room couch, lay them on the floor, and then lie down on those cushions to try to go to sleep each night. I remember looking at those cushions and my first thought was, "People sat on those cushions all day long, and who knows what they deposited on them when they sat on them." My next thought was, "Larry, you are a total fake. Several people sat on those cushions today because they were waiting to come into your office for a counseling session with you, and they paid you to teach them how to become more successful. You are taking money from people for your success coaching, and you can't even coach yourself well enough to make enough money for a proper place to live!" Then I would shake myself out of that negativism by beginning to read a book, listen to a tape or CD, pray, or declare out loud affirmations of truth-based success principles to drown out those negative, destructive thoughts and replace them with positive, nourishing thoughts. Each day I would get better and better at winning this battle going on in my mind.

Then after months of working daily to keep my thoughts right, even while my circumstances seemed hopeless, a breakthrough occurred in my life!

I went to speak to a little group meeting of about twenty people, and after I finished my speech, a person gave to me a piece of paper with a name and phone number scribbled on it. It was a referral to a man and woman who were having a conference the following Friday, and this individual suggested I call them to see if they might want me to come and speak at their conference. The next day while I was making my routine sixty to one hundred phone calls, I found this piece of paper and called these business leaders who had been referred to me. Much to my delight, they agreed to have me come and speak at their conference on that following Friday in July of 1989.

This was the first time that I had spoken in this particular area of business, and I was very excited to learn that there would be over 2000 people in the audience. On Friday I flew to the distant city, and when I entered the meeting room at the conference, I immediately sensed a powerful connection with the leaders and the people. I shared a very simple presentation of four principles that I had been meditating on for weeks. I knew that these principles had been working for me to keep me centered and purpose-driven during my challenging circumstances, and if they were working for me, then I believed with a passion that they would work for anyone who would use them. The group of people at this particular meeting were all independent business owners, so they could relate completely with the principles I shared with them. My presentation was very well received, and I felt very much "On Purpose." Along with the joy of totally loving the experience of being with those people at that conference, I also made enough money that weekend to pay all my bills on time that month! I was so excited about paying my bills that when I arrived back in Detroit that next evening, I took the cushions off the waiting room couch and put those three cushions on my office floor just as I had been doing for almost seven months. But before I laid down to go to sleep, I got out my checkbook and wrote checks to everyone I owed money to, and I also made payments of one thousand and two thousand dollars on some of my credit cards that had gotten way out of control. It felt so wonderful to seal up those envelopes, put postage stamps on them, and stack them in a neat pile on the corner of my desk to be mailed the next morning.

After speaking at that conference, the most that I expected to happen with this particular group was that maybe they might ask me to speak at another one of their conferences some day. What I did not fully realize was that I had just entered a network that connected me with millions of business people. I mentioned in an earlier paragraph of this book about the third of many tapes and CD programs that have been distributed throughout this organization and other affiliated organizations around the world. Well, this particular presentation I shared that weekend in 1989 was recorded on cassette tape, and within a short amount of time the recording of that Friday night talk became the first of many different programs that have been selected to be distributed over the years as a "tape or CD of the week," and 150,000 copies of that one presentation on cassette tape was distributed throughout the world.

A breakthrough occurred, and from that day to this day my life has never been the same. As a direct spin-off of that tape being distributed to 150,000 people and the "word of mouth" referrals that occurred as a result, many leaders throughout this network of hundreds of organizations have asked me to come and speak at their conferences, with thousands of people in attendance. These audiences have ranged from one thousand, five thousand, ten thousand, to sixteen thousand people at a single session. When I add up all the groups that I have been blessed to speak to as direct referrals resulting from that first conference back in 1989, I am humbled to report that during the past seventeen years I have spoken to over one million people, face to face, just within that one business arena alone. All of this happened as a result of one phone call I made on one day during a period of my life when I was sleeping on an office floor.

I don't say this to impress you about me; I say all of this to "impress upon you" that <u>you don't know what day you will pick up your phone, dial a number, and the person who picks up the phone on the other end will become one of the most significant persons in your future life and business.</u>

Keep dialing that phone. The most likely way that you will find "your people" is by making lots of phone calls every day. You may have met the person that you are calling in the grocery store, at church, at a gas station, or through a friend or family member. Value your list of phone contacts just the same way that you would value a sack of gold, because in reality your list of phone numbers is much more valuable. The more times you dial your phone, the more quickly you will find "your most significant people."

Someone may ask, "Larry, back in 1989 how could you go out and talk to groups of people about being successful when you didn't even have enough money to buy a car or put a proper roof over your own head?" The answer to this question is very simple. I had come to a place in my life where I believed that **real truth-success principles will always work if you work them. Those truth-success principles didn't care if I was sleeping on an office floor or in the most expensive house in town. If I faithfully worked those principles, they would work for me and produce positive results.**

Foundational truth-based principles of success will never fail us. The main ingredients needed on our part are persistence and consistency. Simply stated, "If you ask you will receive, if you seek you will find, if you knock it will be opened to you".

The key point here is to not reject yourself just because things do not seem to be going as well as you would like them to at any particular season of life. When we reject ourselves and settle for a comfort zone existence instead of going for the next higher level, the very fact that we have rejected the larger vision for our life will weaken our faith and automatically disqualify us from being able to sustain the mental and emotional energy required to continue to ask, seek and knock. Sometimes we must "speak of things that be not, as though they are". This may seem crazy to some people, but it is often the only way to keep believing and to keep yourself in a place of active faith on those days when things don't seem to be going in the right direction, and it may even seem that no matter how hard you work, you are still getting nowhere.

In the play *Man of La Mancha* there is a line that has always meant a lot to me: "It is madness to accept reality as it is, rather than as it should be!"

Many days it will take deliberate effort and action to stay positive and to not give in to the temptation to reject ourselves. We will have to practice a lot of thought-replacement and thought-exchange to keep our faith going in the right direction. Someone who has never read any of my books or heard me speak may ask, "What is thought-replacement and thought-exchange?" Thought-replacement is the daily practice of replacing the negative thoughts and negative self-talk that we have previously let into our minds and hearts with positive truth-based thoughts. Everything that is alive and healthy has a waste elimination system that is functioning properly. As we bring in the positive truth-based thoughts, we will automatically flush out of our minds and hearts the negative self-talk thoughts. Thought-exchange is the daily practice of exchanging or current positive thoughts with higher-level truth-based principle laws. In other words, to practice thought-exchange we must be willing to be humble enough to even exchange what we thought was "the complete truth". When we discover that we were operating with a limited view and in fact, "the real, more complete truth" was actually on a higher level than the lower level that we had previously been operating and thinking on, we quickly and completely exchange our previous thoughts with the more replete truth-based thoughts that we have newly discovered. "As a man or woman thinketh, so they shall be". As we continue to daily upgrade our collection of thoughts, our upgraded thoughts will then eventually change our philosophy about different areas of life. This change in philosophy will automatically change our reality, and this change in our reality ("As your Faith is, so it will be unto you") will finally be manifested in the form of an upgraded life experience. But first, we have to hold the right thoughts, the right vision, and the right faith for a period of time while we can't yet see the manifested vision with our physical eyes. In your heart, in the "real you", you can know, that you know, that you know, even before there is any outward evidence to prove the vision of what you know is the highest dream-purpose for your life. The law of faith requires that we first must "know it" and "see it" on the inside of us, and then it will be manifested on the outside in the world where the five senses can observe it. Some people say, "I'll believe it, when I see it", but the Now-Faith method of operation is "When you believe it, then you will see it"! Now-Faith is "the substance of things hoped for and the evidence of things not seen". If you will resist the temptation to reject your self and your dream-purpose and hold the right vision long enough, it will become an outwardly manifested reality.

It works if you work it

Today I can unashamedly and passionately go out to tell other people about truth-success-principles, as I did back in 1989, simply because I know that throughout history they had been proven to be 100% reliable. Someone may ask, "But Larry, back in 1989, how did you overcome the tendency to feel like a hypocrite and reject yourself? You were not looking very successful if someone would see you sleeping on that office floor." The answer to this is very simple as well. At times I was certainly tempted to feel like a total hypocrite or a fraud, but then, as I kept renewing my thoughts, I would realize that it would be very presumptuous of me to think that the age-old, tested, tried, and true foundational principles of success needed me to validate them, or that somehow they would become weaker or stronger depending on what my life circumstances, or anyone else's, happen to be at any given moment in time. I kept myself centered on the fact that **the truth-faith-based-success-principles that really work are based on laws that are just as real and reliable as the law of gravity and the law that light always dispels the darkness. When you drop something with any weight to it, it falls downward, and when the lights come on in a dark room the darkness**

always leaves. Nobody will debate these laws because they have been proven by life experience enough times to remove all doubt about their validity. These laws will work just as well for a person who is presently living in an office as they will work for a person living in a multi-million dollar mansion.

By keeping my mind continually renewed and my heart continually reassured of this truth, I was able to stay in a place mentally, spiritually, and emotionally where I knew that decreeing these laws to be true was not only something that I could share with others and speak about with the highest level of integrity, but I was also actually speaking creative words that would be manifested by recreating my life as I was helping other people recreate their lives as well. **I settled it in my heart and mind that these laws could never become any more true, powerful, or potent than they already are and that they will work every time when you take complete action and work them properly. They do not depend on me or anybody else to validate them or decide whether they will keep working and still be true. They will work for anyone who really works them, anywhere, all the time, and that's it...period.**

Reading the biographies of successful purpose-driven people historically proves that some of the people who accomplished the greatest things were also people who started out with what seemed to be the greatest disadvantages.

So even if our circumstances are not what we want them to be, we can still go out and help other people become a success. **If we share success principles with enough other people, and if we can help enough other people get to their next higher level, then we will get pushed up to our next higher level as an automatic result of our operating in the "law of reciprocity," and our circumstances will improve accordingly.**

I am not going to go through a long list of these laws and principles because I feel I should keep this part of this book as brief and to the point as possible. But I believe that it is beneficial for us to take a deeper look at this "law of reciprocity." Again, just like the *law of gravity,* this law will always work when you work it. The "law of reciprocity," is also stated: "As you give, so you will receive." You have to plant if you want to reap a harvest. You have to be willing to give some love to someone else if you want to receive love. If you want peace, you will have to give up worrying. If we want success, we will have to give up the habits that have caused us to fail in the past. If we want more money, we will have to give or invest some money first.

This includes the reality which I mentioned earlier that most of the time you and I will have to start giving "on faith" even when we haven't received any outward sign that anything is changing for the positive. Also, we have to use wisdom as we decide where to give and who to give to. Oftentimes it is a good idea to counsel with our mentor about where and to whom we should give our seeds of faith to. Operating with good discernment concerning where we invest our time, energy, and substance will keep us in alignment with the *law of good stewardship,* which, to paraphrase it in simple language, states, "He or she who is found faithful when given authority to receive a little amount of any type of blessing in life, will ultimately be given favor and authority to receive much in an abundant, overflowing fashion," even to the point where "…blessings will come upon us and overtake us" in ways and quantities that are "…beyond what we could even ask or think" and on higher levels than what we could have even imagined were possible.

Well, again I have to discipline myself here to stop talking about these laws, or this book may never end!!!

It is amazing to look back and realize all the great things that have happened which had their origin in that one phone call out of thousands of phone calls I had made while I was sleeping on that office floor.

Fast forwarding my "life movie" I have to pinch myself to make sure I am not dreaming as I review what has happened since the day I first made the shift to the national speaking area, then spoke to that group of 2000 people, the first distribution of 150,000 tapes and CDs, and then called that great business leader for the twenty-second time, which resulted in my having the privilege of speaking to those 45, 000 people in one month.

I have spoken to many different kinds of audiences and in many different niche markets over the years. But as I think of the blessing of being privileged to speak live and face-to-face to over one million people in the United States, throughout Europe, Canada, South Africa, and in many other locations all around the world as a result of working within this one business niche market. I also have a heart filled with gratitude that to date, over three quarters of a million audio copies of my presentations have been distributed on "tape and CDs of the week" programs just in this one niche market and this number will most likely exceed one million copies of tapes and CDs in the years to come. In addition, hundreds of thousands of copies of my books have been distributed through "book of the month" programs exclusively through this same one niche market. In fact, my sense of urgency to get my first book written was mainly due to the fact that I knew there was a hunger for what I was sharing, and I believed that tens of thousands of copies would immediately be purchased as soon as I got that first book written. So it is humbling and with an awesome sense of gratitude that I realize that I owe a lot to the many great leaders who have been a blessing to me and have promoted my work over the years, both in this one niche market and in all of the other, businesses, organizations, and groups that I have had the privilege to work with.

Please understand the place that I am coming from in my heart as I tell you about these amazing blessings. **My desire here, is to "drive home the point" to you and to me that it is not our present circumstances that are the greatest determining factors of how high we can go in life...it is whether you and I can keep our thoughts right and stay purpose-driven and continue to be laser focused on truth-success-principles, even in the toughest times.** That is what makes the difference in whether we will or will not go to our next higher level and enjoy freedom in every area of our lives.

Is it important that we make lots of phone calls and talk to lots of people while building any vision, mission, or business? YES!! YES!! YES!! "We must talk to the many to find the few who we were meant to be with all along." Isn't it exciting to know that if we will continue consistently for a long enough period of time to "talk to the many to find the few," there will come a time when the few we find will then go out to find "the many"!! But, first we must pay the price upfront and "talk to the many." I am not just talking about an unproven theory here. I made thousands of phone calls before getting to that one phone call while sleeping on the office floor in 1989, and then made those twenty-two phone calls to another man and many, many other phone calls to more and more people on a daily and weekly basis.

Was it worth it to face all of the potential rejection that came along with all of those phone calls and meetings with all of those people? The answer to that question is Yes, Yes, Yes, and an infinite number of Yeses...

I am very humbled by all of this blessing because I know that I am no more special than anyone else. If anyone is willing to overcome the same amount of delayed gratification and perceived rejection that I have overcome throughout the years, there is no doubt that **anyone**...in their sphere of activity and in the niche that they are purposed to work in...**anyone** could receive much, much more than I have been blessed with.

Let me present a challenge to you and to me right here. I will accept this challenge right along with you because I know that we have all just scratched the surface of what is actually possible for us. The greatest leaders that I have been privileged to know are all people who readily admit that they have not yet "arrived" or hit their highest level. We have greater mountains to climb and higher levels to soar to and many more people that we can still be a blessing to by helping them get to a higher level of freedom in their lives.

I really believe that most people give up way too easily.

So here is the challenge: Let's go and get out that list of people that we have called five or ten times and then given up on. If you don't have a list, then go through your files or address book and make a list. Sit down and think about all of the people you have called to join you in business or whatever vision you are passionate about, but after a few tries you felt rejected and never called them back. Now you don't have to be as crazy as I am and call twenty-two times, but I would encourage you to pick up the phone and start calling these people again until they either say, "Yes" or "Don't call me any more"!

From my experience, every time I have gotten my list out and called people who did not respond positively to me in the past, I have ALWAYS found that some of those people were now at a different place in life and were thinking differently than they were the last time I had talked with them. And the fact that they had come to a different place in life, with different priorities, now caused them to react more positively to me. Often these people, whom I called after not talking with them for six months, a year, or even several years, became some of the strongest supporters and blessings in my life and business after I reconnected with them.

Someone might say, "Well, I don't want to bug people and become a nuisance." Well, please remember that if we are careful to be kind and patient while we are "bugging" those people, and if we keep on laying on one light layer at a time, the people we contact will most likely develop a deep respect for us because we are being persistent without being pushy.

You may not end up speaking to 45,000 people in one month or experience the same blessings that I have personally enjoyed, but in your sphere of activity, you will have some breakthroughs that will be just as big, and maybe even bigger, in relation to what you are purposed to do in life. Over time you will be able to receive something just as important and valuable to you in context with your goals and your vision in life.

True success never goes on sale. You always have to pay full price, but the blessings that you will receive after you have paid the price will pay off for years to come in residual and compounding proportions.

Sometimes it's not rejection – it's just a matter of timing

Have you ever experienced a time when you felt that someone was rejecting you and the main reason for their not responding positively to you sounded something like this: "I would like to say yes, but the timing is just not good for me right now"? It is true that this is one of the most commonly used "polite brush-off lines," but it is vital that we also remember that timing plays a major part in every major decision-making process.

While understanding that timing is very important, we have also all had people try to brush us off with the "timing excuse." when we may have known that whatever they were really thinking had very little to do with their concern about proper synchronicity.

Though there are those times when you just know that you would be wasting your breath to continue talking to a specific person, I have found that frequently it doesn't pay to write people off just because they say they have some degree of caution about the timing of what I am proposing.

I can speak from personal experience that when a person tells me that "timing" is the main obstacle to their agreeing to my proposal, in most cases this was not a red light or a stop sign but rather a blinking yellow light indicating that I needed to slow down, look around in all directions, and then proceed to move forward with a desire to discover how to adjust the timing so that it would work for them.

Often the bigger the deal is or the larger the reward that we will eventually be blessed with, the more of a need there will be for us to be patient and keep moving forward even in the face of one delay after another.

Shortly after I had just finished writing my first book, "The Resilient Power Of Purpose" (formerly titled: "How To Be Purpose Driven") in the late 1990s, someone told me about a company that had bought 20,000 of their books in one single order. I was making phone calls every day to people who would end up buying 50, 100, 500, or even

1000 books in one single order, but this 20,000 in one order sounded amazing to me! The 20,000 books would be printed and just shipped directly from my printing company to the client in one truckload, and then the client would distribute the books to 20,000 separate customers.

After getting the contact information for this company, I got in contact with them and sent them a sample copy of my book. I then proceeded to follow up with phone calls to see if they had reviewed it. Sixteen phone calls later I finally heard the words "Yes, we have finished reviewing your book." These words were quickly followed by another phrase: "We like your book, but the timing is just not right for us to use it at the moment".

I continued to call this company, and as I kept careful records of each time I called them, I started to wonder if maybe the timing would never be right. It got a little embarrassing at times, but I continued to keep asking the same person the same question as I proceeded to call them every seven to fourteen days for about nine months.

Each time I called, I would ask basically the same question: "How does the timing look for my book to be used by your company?" I tried to be creative so that I didn't say those same exact words in that exact order every time I called. But when I did not hear the "yes" I was waiting for, I would ask, "When can I call you back to check with you again?" They would usually say, "Our next meeting for book reviews is next week or in two weeks," so I would make a note on my calendar to call them back on a certain date.

After thirty-one more phone calls I dialed one more time and asked the same question. Much to my surprise I heard these words, "You know what, Larry, we just had a meeting yesterday, and everyone at the meeting agreed that this would be the perfect time to use your book! I will fax you a Purchase Order this afternoon for 20,000 copies, and we would like them to be delivered to us in five weeks."!!!

Needless to say I was "flying high" that day. But when you do the arithmetic on that book deal, I had called them a total forty-seven times, and on about 60% of those calls I got the same response: "The timing isn't right".

I realize most people would have stopped calling them long before the forty-seventh time, but I guess most of the time I just don't know when to quit! If I get it in my head and in my heart that I want something and it is part of my purpose to receive it, I lose all perspective on what is traditionally considered to be reasonable, and I keeping moving, even if it seems to be one inch at a time. After all, if they didn't want me to bother them anymore, they would have just flat out told me "no", wouldn't they?

Yes, amazingly enough, someone could say "The timing is not right at this moment" for thirty-one consecutive times and still that was never an actual rejection! All it meant was that the timing TRULY was not exactly right until the thirty-second call.

After I wrote my second book, I sent it to this same company, and guess what? That's right; I got the same response: "The timing is not exactly right for your book at this moment". I received this same response over and over with the second book, and then on the day when the timing was suddenly perfect for my second book, "The Magic Is In The Extra Mile", I received another huge book order.

I may have doubted quite a few times whether they would ever buy the first book, but I had very little doubt that eventually my second book would fit their needs and at some point the timing would be right. A major reason why I had this increased confidence the second time around was because I had paid the price to go beyond the temptation to feel rejected while selling the first book. **All of the growth that we will experience during a present period of persistence will give us added confidence in our future dealings.**

Timing may not be everything, but it is a big part of many decisions. If you don't quit, if you refuse to give up, you will find that with some of your greatest break-throughs--once you get the ball rolling--<u>it truly is,</u> to a great extent, just a matter of time, persistence, and repetition on your part.

If you will get out that list of people that you have already called five, eight, or even ten times and call them one more time, or call them ten or twenty more times, I guarantee that some of them will eventually say "yes". You will look back on some of those yes's, and you will say to yourself, "I'm so glad I didn't quit calling them. I'm so glad I didn't see their delays as a rejection. These have turned out to be some of the greatest blessings of my entire life!"

Here is a sideline note that I have found helpful. If you call some people five or ten times over a short period of time, and you keep getting their voice mail, it is usually best to not leave a message every time you call. But, over a period of time, if you do find it necessary to leave several voice mails before being able to connect with them, it is best to not mention the previous voice messages you left. Keep your voice light and positive, and leave every voice mail as though it were the very first one that you have left since you last talked with them in person.

Remember, you don't have to win them all, but if you're going to win any, you have to have the attitude that if you give up and quit, you will never know what great potential was actually possible. The fact is, if you take massive action and you don't quit, you're going to get where you want to be!

After you have paid the price to create momentum – IT GETS A LOT EASIER

The great news is that after you have spent a period of time making twenty, thirty, fifty or more phone calls a day and have attended many face-to-face meetings with people, you will have created enough momentum that you can start to see the "snowball effect" take over.

When you first launch your pursuit, you will begin to build a base by calling many people every day, which will eventually result in your meeting with more and more people each week. At first it is not uncommon for a fair number of the phone calls or meetings to end with less than a definite "yes" from the person or people you are sharing your vision with. At first it may seem like you are rolling the snowball uphill with lots of effort and possibly little manifested progress. But then, after enough days of consistent action, you can actually feel when the shift takes place and you have crowned the peak of the mountain. At that point the snowball starts to roll downhill, picking up more and more speed and getting bigger and bigger as each day's aggregate phone calls and meetings are added to the quantity of the snowball or, in this case, the "phone call and meeting ball."

Each day you create greater momentum than the previous day, and when you have put enough contacts out there, it starts coming back. And when what you've been putting out there starts to come back, it is indeed a beautiful thing to behold.

Once you have operated in alignment with the "**You must talk to the many, to find the few**" law for enough consecutive days, you will start to reap consistent rewards in proportion to the amount of seeds you have planted. Of course, for you to be able to "pay the price" of massive consistent action to talk to "the many", you will have also had to "pay the price" to keep your thoughts right, which will enable you to flow in the right kind of attracting charisma. You will find that there will come a time when your role will change. Instead of spending all of your time making outbound phone calls, much of your time will be invested in returning all the phone calls that come pouring in.

Daily persistence is the key here. If you keep your daily momentum up at a high enough pitch…it will almost seem like miracles start to happen. There is an awesome sense of fulfillment and expectancy when you have paid enough of a price for a long enough time. It is an amazing faith building experience when the roles reverse and you get to the point where people actually start to pursue you, instead of you having to pursue them!

To see this happen you have to get the "daily thing" down right and stick with it. I say it this way, "You have to do at least enough each day to be able to keep your plane up in the air."

Doing enough every day
to keep your plane up in the air

As a jet plane lifts off the runway and starts its ascent, you will notice that the engines seem to be roaring at full power. However, I have talked with a number of pilots about this, and they have told me that the engines are not maxed out at full throttle during take-off. I think this is a very comforting fact. It is always nice to know that they still have some extra power available if it is needed. But as you listen to those engines roar, it is still quite obvious that they are pushing them pretty hard when they first take off.

When the plane gets up to a few thousand feet, the pilot or the plane's automated system backs those engines off, and at about ten thousand feet the engines' thrust is often backed off even more. When the jet gets to the designated cruising altitude those engines are often backed off to the point that, in some of the larger jets, you can hardly even hear the engines running when you're cruising at an altitude of thirty or forty thousand feet.

The principle here is that "it always takes a lot less energy to keep the momentum going than it takes to get it started'

In context with whatever your pursuit is, whatever vision you are working on, or whatever business you are building, as a bare minimum **it is in your best interest to make sure that you are taking enough massive action, that at the very least, you are creating enough momentum each day to keep your dream-purpose-vision-mission jet plane up in the air. Even if you didn't break any records in production on any one particular day, if you have merely kept your plane up in the air, then you have something to be very proud of. You have kept the law of momentum working in your favor.**

If the opposite happens, and you have a start-and-stop quality to your daily consistency or, in this case, we should call it your daily <u>inconsistency</u>, then you will most likely become exhausted and quit after a short amount of time. Why? Because you could not keep your mental and emotional energy high enough and strong enough to maintain the momentum that is needed to keep moving forward.

Think about it. Let's say that you are building your business, and for the first six days of the month everything is going great. You have been making lots of phone calls and lots of appointments to meet with people, and sales volume is right on track with your goals, which, of course is a direct result of your daily consistent action. You look at the early success of your month in progress and say to yourself, "I have been working so hard, I deserve a break", so you decide to take a day off.

There is nothing wrong with taking a day off every once in a while, but in this case one day turns into two, three, and finally six days off, and you have not made one phone call or set up one meeting, and things slow down to the point where you have "landed your plane." Now you see that you are approaching the middle of the month and you are no longer on target to meet your monthly goals. So you taxi your vision or business plane down the runway and build enough speed to once again take off.

For the second time that month you have put out the tremendous amount of energy required to get your plane back up in the air and are producing again. About the third week of the month you look outside and say, "Wow, what a beautiful sunny day. This could be the last good day of weather before winter sets in. I'd better get that yard work done" So, one day of cutting grass and weeding the flower gardens becomes two, three, and then four days, and guess what? Yep, that's right; you look around and realize that you have once again landed your plane.

You realize that you only have six days left of that month, and if you don't make something happen quickly, you are going to have a miserable "business month's end". So what do you do? You rev up your mental and emotional engines, and down the runway you go. Once again you put every last ounce of energy you have left into getting that plane back up in the air again. Very possibly you do meet the minimum goal that you have set for that month, but how do you feel? After two landings and the extreme energy output of three ground-level takeoffs, you will be flat worn out.

You could very possibly think to yourself, "I just don't

know if I have *what it takes* to be a success at this. Other people may be cut out for this kind of work, but as for me, this is way too energy draining and way too stressful." This is often the time when a person will quit and give up on their vision of a better life or a higher level of freedom, and they will decide to settle for a lower level and a comfort zone existence that will not require that they experience much growth at all.

The truth is that everyone has *what it takes*. But even if you or I find our perfect niche to work in and have a great support team working with us, if we don't keep the law of "daily momentum" working in our favor, we will probably sooner or later become overwhelmed and quit.

Here is what I call a "Shift Point': A shift point is a statement of truth that causes a shift in our hearts and minds. Shift Point: **"Most people do not forfeit their next higher level of success or freedom because they don't want it. Almost everyone wants it. Most people stop working on going to their next higher level because they have simply become too mentally and emotionally depleted to have the faith and energy to take the next step. So they give up and quit before their next higher level is manifested."**

It is wonderful to know that you and I don't have to allow ourselves to get to that kind of weakened mental and emotional state. We can keep our daily purpose-driven truth-based principle intake level high enough by renewing our thoughts and also put out the energy it takes to make all of the contacts and do all of the work we need to complete while still keep our plane up in the air. We can do all this and still have lots of mental and emotional energy left over to invest in those who deserve and need our mentoring.

Whether we will be able to be a great leader will be

determined to a great extent by how well we are able to keep our own personal power-base solid and strong.

To lead others and mentor others, we need to stay in a place where our spiritual, mental, and emotional state is maintained with a high enough level of faith and belief that we will be able to help those who come to us with their belief level at zero or even below zero. As we keep our *daily momentum* right, it gets easier for us to keep our personal stamina strong enough that we are no longer anxious or worried about trying to *keep it together* ourselves. When we know that we have paid the price to "step over this line, and we have gone beyond the point of no return," then we can wisely and generously share our extra energy by spending time developing other leaders.

Developing a group of leaders is one of the greatest keys to building a huge vision, mission, or business. Here is a principle-based <u>leadership shift point</u>: **"If you want to build a small vision, mission, or business, then build something where it all depends on you to get things done. If you want to build a huge vision, mission, or business, then you must develop leaders who will add their faith and efforts to yours"**.

The higher you fly, the easier it can get!!

I have heard people say, "I would not want to become too successful because life would become too hard to deal with." If we become successful by practicing the right principles and laws, it is actually the opposite of this that we find to be true. The more successful you become and the higher that you fly, it should actually become easier and easier for you to maintain and increase your momentum.

I was on a plane a few days ago, and I heard the pilot say something I had never heard before. During the flight, the turbulence was pretty extreme, and the pilots had to continually switch altitudes to try to find a smoother place to fly. Finally the voice of one of the pilots came over the P.A. system telling us that he had tried 15,000 feet, 12,000 feet, 8,000 feet, and had to finally go down to between 5,000 and 6,000 feet for the rest of the flight.

We were flying over a body of water, and as we flew the pilot gave us a geography lesson about the different islands we could see below us and added other interesting geographical information. After the plane had landed, I was standing at the front of the plane waiting to get off when two pilots came out of the flight deck. I asked them, "Which one of you gave us that great geography lesson while we were up in the air?" One of the two pilots stepped forward and said "That was me. We don't get to fly that low very often, and it was fun to be able to see everything so clearly." Then he added this sentence. "One of the main reasons we don't usually fly that low is that we use up much more fuel when we fly at lower altitudes. The air up at higher altitudes is much thinner and offers much less resistance against the plane, but the lower we go in altitude, the thicker the air becomes, and that greater resistance causes us to burn more fuel!"

When I heard him say that I thought to myself, "Wow, that is just like going to a higher level of success. If you keep your success-plane at a lower altitude, it will be hard to keep things going because you will burn up way too much energy and you will finally feel too exhausted to continue. But if you keep your success-plane flying at higher and higher altitudes, it will actually get easier and easier the higher you go.

Two wonderful additional benefits you will be blessed with while flying at higher levels of success are that you will be able to associate with other nourishing high-flying people and you will be avoiding the low-flying toxic people. Most of the negative-energy draining people in life are usually "low-flyers". So an automatic benefit of being a "high flyer" is that you will be up there with a group of people who are very inspiring to be around!

Whatever the price that you will have to pay to daily make sure you are keeping your plane high up in the ether, above the negative quagmire of the common-thinking masses, it will pay huge rewards back to you in life. This will allow you to live a freer life with greater momentum and less stress! Flying high is a beautiful way to live and do business!

Chapter

6

Keep Your Purpose Level Higher Than The Challenge Level

When we talk about "purpose," there is a tendency to selectively think of people like Mother Theresa, Gandhi, Martin Luther King Jr., or other *bigger than life* historical characters. We can readily accept that they had a great purpose in life, but what about you and me? In order for you to be able to stay purpose-driven on a daily basis, you must find what I call your "personal purpose."

The most clear and accurate way to crystallize what your "personal purpose" is to find the top reasons for why you <u>must</u> go to your next higher level. **Your reasons are your purpose.** As I have worked to help thousands of people to stay purpose-driven over the years, I have found that it is best for individuals to identify the top five reasons that "drive them" or "turn them on" in context with going to their next higher level.

Why five reasons? Because if we, at the very least, find the top five reasons, we will usually have found our number one reason somewhere in the "Top Five." When sorting out our reasons, often what we first thought to be reason number three or reason number four will later be revealed as actually our number one reason. The deeper we dig and the further we go, the more we will be enlightened as to what our real number one driving reason is for us personally. The number one reason is often buried under so much excess baggage of negative thinking we have collected throughout our lives that it may take a lot of soul searching to uncover the true number one reason.

Most people have written off their highest dream-life as not really being possible to attain, and their main reason for getting to that dream-life was often buried along with the dream. Someone once said, "Most people die by the age of twenty-five or thirty. They just don't get buried until they are seventy or eighty." So even though the highest level of purpose-driven momentum will come from knowing your number one reason, it is in your best interest to find the "Top Five" reasons why you *must* get to your next higher level.

The word <u>must</u> is a key word in this process. We are not talking here about finding five reasons why it would be just good or nice to get to the next higher level. We are looking for the <u>top</u> five most important reasons, the most life-changing reasons that are not optional but are absolutely necessary for achieving total freedom in every area of our lives--spiritual, relational, mental, financial, etc.

If you know the real top five reasons for why you <u>must</u> get to your next higher level, and if you have discovered how to stay focused on those top five reasons every day, you will be able to keep your *purpose level* high. The higher you are able to keep your *purpose level*, the less influence the challenges of life will have to be able to affect you.

If you compare your *purpose level* vs. your *challenge level* on a scale from one to ten, whichever you find to be higher will determine your resiliency level.

To illustrate this point, first think about the next higher level that you want to go to in your vision, your business, or your mission in life. Now just for an example's sake, let's say that on a scale from one to ten, for you to be able to rise above the level where you are right now and move up to your next higher level, the challenge level is at five. If the challenge level is at five and you wake up one morning and your *purpose level*, or in other words, "your ability to focus on your top five reasons" is at a level of two on a scale from one to ten, let me ask you a question.

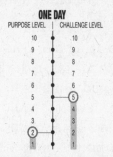

If the challenge level is at five and your purpose level is at two, how will you feel that particular day about getting your list of people out and dialing the phone or setting up meetings with them? With a purpose level of two and a challenge level of five, you or I will probably not want to pick up the phone. In fact, we might just want to pull the covers over our head and go back to sleep!

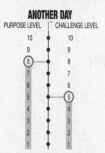

Now for another example, let's say that you wake up on another day and your purpose level is at an eight and the challenge level is at a five. How do you feel this day about making the phone calls and meeting with the people? With a purpose level of eight or nine and a challenge level of five, you are "locked and loaded," charged up and ready to go. You can start dialing the phone with confidence and flow in positive-attracting charisma.

What was the difference from one day to the next? Did the challenge level change? No, the challenge level was at five on both days. The only thing that changed was your "purpose level" or your ability to focus on those top five reasons.

Obviously we are using numbers on a scale from one to ten strictly as a way to visualize the challenge level vs. our purpose level. If we had a meter to measure our purpose level vs. the challenge level, it would be very similar to the procedure used to check a car battery to see if it is sustaining a strong enough power output to be able to start the car's engine. If we let our car sit unused for a long enough period of time, the battery will slowly lose its charge, and when we try to start the car, it won't start. To fix this problem, we often can simply hook the battery up to a battery charger until the battery is back up to the level of power needed to start the engine.

Even though we do not have an actual external device to measure our *purpose-driven-level*, we do have an internal device. You can access this internal device by asking yourself one simple question: "Today, are there any challenges that could cause me to lose faith and quit pursuing the next higher level of my dream-purpose?" If from the deepest part of your heart your honest answer to this question is "yes," then you know at that moment your purpose level is lower than the challenge level. If your answer to that question is a heart-honest, absolute "no," then you know that your purpose level at that moment is higher than any challenge level you will face.

Another way to gauge how strong your purpose level

is to check yourself to see if mentally and emotionally you are under the spell of any fears, feelings of unworthiness, insecurities, etc. If you are being affected by these negative influences, then you know that your purpose level is too low. When our purpose level is high enough, we will repel fears, feelings of unworthiness, insecurities, and the like, and they will bounce off of us like a Ping-Pong ball bouncing off the table.

We obviously don't want to create any unnecessary challenges or adversities, but if you study the life of massively successful people, you will find that they did not become massively successful in any area of life because they spent a lot of time trying to avoided challenges and adversity. In fact, those who become massively successful very often face greater challenges and adversity than others who have settled for a lower-level comfort-zone existence. The people who become massively successful do so by maintaining a strong enough and big enough dream-purpose-reality so that any challenge or adversity will look smaller in comparison.

The minimum challenge-level is made up of whatever the required challenges are that you must overcome to make your personal dream-purpose a reality. This is non-negotiable. Someone may say, "I want to get to my next higher level, but I want to do it without having any challenges!" Well, that would be nice, but that is not the way success works. **A plane cannot fly without the resistance of air, and the challenges in our lives are often what cause us to grow stronger and fly higher.**

Eagles sense a storm before the storm moves in, and they know how to use the beginning winds of a storm to their advantage. When an eagle senses that a storm is brewing, it simply cups its' wings to catch a ride on the first winds and the beginning turbulence of a storm.

Using this technique causes the eagle to be driven up higher, up where that sun is shining!

You and I have to be willing to look at the challenge level of five or six or whatever it may be, and we have to decide that we are willing to pay the price of the challenge and then just move forward with a strong sense of purpose. To think that we are going to achieve anything of real worth without facing any challenges or some form of adversity is just a form of fantasy that weakens our resiliency.

If you take a look at someone who has already achieved something similar to what you are setting out to accomplish, you will be able to get a pretty good idea of the challenges you may have to be willing to overcome if you want to get to the same higher level that person has risen to. Of course you may not be faced with the same set of challenges this other person faced, but at least you will have a *ball park* idea of how you need to "count the cost" and what price you will have to be willing to pay.

If you can find an easier route—without compromising your dream-purpose--to get to that higher level, then all the better. But it's better to go in being willing to pay a higher price than you ultimately will have to pay and find out that it will be less, rather than to go in thinking it will be less and then find out it is much more of a stretch than you thought it would be.

Driving along a particular road you may have noticed, as I have, a house that is obviously only halfway through the building process and remains that way for years. When I see this, I often wonder if the person who started building the house may have underestimated the actual cost to finish the house and therefore could not complete the project. **When it comes to going to the next higher level of our dream–purpose, a wise builder predetermines to be pre-**

pared and willing to pay an even higher price than what is initially obvious.

After we have determined the minimum and maximum challenges of getting to our next higher level, it is best to spend our energy in concentrating on the positive vision of what we want, rather than spending our precious energy worrying about challenges.

Just get it fixed in your heart that you are willing to face whatever obstacles you may encounter and move on to be proactive with at sense of urgency, an attitude of gratitude, and a heart filled with faith.

Sometimes being *willing* to face a challenge does not mean that you will have to actually go through it. For example, I have been at different points in life where I was ready to take on a big challenge, and then one of my mentors would give me a valuable piece of advice and would counsel me in a direction that helped me to dissolve the challenge quickly and easily, just as you would melt an ice cube in a microwave oven!

Again, let me reiterate, your ability to focus on the top five reasons of WHY YOU MUST get to your next higher level will equal your purpose-level, and your purpose-level will equal your level of resiliency.

Let's go deeper here to become totally clear on what it means to find our top five reasons. These are generally not the first five reasons that come to our mind. You may need to go sit down and just stare at the wall and think for a few hours to finally find the real "Top Five" reasons that will be the purpose strong enough to drive you through any challenge or obstacle. In a practical sense, finding these top five reasons is what truly being purpose-driven is all about.

If you know your biggest WHY for living and WHY

you want to achieve your next higher level, then you will have an overcoming spirit, which will cause you to do WHATEVER is necessary to break through to countless victories in life and business!

Someone may ask, "How do I know if I have found my TOP FIVE reasons?" The answer to this is very simple. "If you write your five reasons on a piece of paper, and every time you look at those five reason they always, without fail, drive you into action to make more phone calls or do some other action-oriented activity that will move you forward, then you know that you have found your TOP FIVE. But, if you write five reasons on a piece of paper, and when you read them, they do not always drive you into action, then you know that you have not yet found your "Top Five" reasons. The reasons you have written down may be five real reasons, but they are not the TOP FIVE. Your TOP FIVE most important reasons will never fail to ALWAYS drive you into action.

If you spend three hours in a chair just thinking about your reasons and you finally find your Top Five, then that would be three of the most profitable hours you have ever invested.

Again, let's remember that some of your top five reasons may have become buried deep inside you over the years. It is not always easy to find them, especially if they have been hidden underneath, or mixed in with, negative self-talk thoughts.

Here is a process you can use to find or rediscover your top five reasons. Sit at a table or desk with five sheets of paper. As you visualize the next higher level that you want to go to in your life or in your business, begin to write on the first sheet of paper every reason that comes to your mind of why you MUST get to that next higher level. Just let your mind and heart run wild. Even if some of the reasons seem similar to some of the other reasons you have already written down, don't worry about that. Write that reason down anyway. Also, do not make any effort to prioritize the reasons or rethink the reasons while you are writing them on this first sheet of paper. At this phase of the process, just keep writing as many reasons as fast as you can, until you run out of reasons.

Next, look over your list of reasons to see if some of the reasons will jar your thinking and cause you to think of even more reasons. As you think of more reasons, add them to the end of your list. By now you may have a list with eighty, a hundred, or maybe even more reasons. Some of the reasons will be spiritual reasons, family reasons, financial freedom reasons, lifestyle reasons, etc.

Next, put a blank sheet of paper next to the list you have just created. Read down your first list and out of the eighty or more reasons on your first sheet of paper, pick out the Top Fifty reasons and write those fifty most important reasons on your second sheet of paper. Then read through the second list of fifty reasons and pick out the Top Twenty reasons from that second list and write those Top Twenty reasons on a third sheet of paper. From the third sheet, pick out your ten most important reasons and write your Top Ten on the fourth sheet of paper. Then read the reasons on the Top Ten sheet and pick out your Top Five and write those reasons on the fifth sheet of paper.

These Top Five reasons that you have located are priceless and can provide you with the inspiration that will drive you to any height that you are purposed to go to. These Top Five reasons are the driving force that can propel you to overcome a mountain of adversity and to achieve all of the personal, spiritual, relationship, and financial freedom that you desire.

You may have noticed that I said these Top Five can drive/propel you, not that they will drive/propel you. The reason I used the word "can" instead of "will" is that finding the Top Five is only the first step. If you set this sheet of paper aside and never look at it again, these reasons will fade into the background of your mind and most likely, once again, will get buried under a bunch of other thoughts. You can stay in a place spiritually, mentally, and emotionally where you are guaranteed that these Top Five will always drive/propel you without fail. But how consistently and powerfully they will inspire you and keep you purpose-driven will depend on how strongly and continually you discipline yourself to focus on them, meditate on them, and keep them at the forefront of your mind and heart each day.

In a business sense, these Top Five reasons can be worth millions of dollars. In a personal sense, the peace, fulfilling relationships, and family blessings that you can achieve are virtually priceless.

So here is the foundational, truth-based success principle that we can always rely on to work anytime and anywhere: **"If you can, at all times, keep your purpose level higher than your challenge level, then you will always have the purpose-driven power to overcome challenges and do whatever it takes to get to your next higher level."** You literally will become unstoppable!

Someone may say, "Well, if the challenge level is five, then I just need to keep my purpose level at six and I'll be ok." Technically, I guess that this is true, but it would be safer to keep your purpose level at an eight or a nine, so if something discouraging happens that day and you drop down a couple of points, then you will still be at a purpose level of six or seven, and you will be able to keep going. If your purpose level is at six and the challenge-level is at five when something discouraging happens, it might knock you down to being able to focus on a purpose-level of only three or four. If this happens, most likely you will get knocked out of the game for a while until you can get your purpose level back up again. So it is better to do some extra work at the front end to make sure that your purpose-level is at a good, solid three or four points higher than the challenge-level. This will assure that you will be able to triumph over any turbulence or adversity that may hit you at any given time.

Knowing...that all things are working together for your good

I have been using numbers in the last several paragraphs to illustrate the correlation between your purpose level vs. the challenge level. But what it really gets down to at a heart level is having a strong enough "knowing" that you will be able to overcome doubts, fears, feelings of rejection, or any other negative influences that may try to attach themselves to you.

We all know the difference between a strong "mental immune system" and a weak one. **If our "mental immune system" is strong, we know that when we are attacked by the arrows of negative thoughts, most of these imposters will just dissolve in the positive ether that surrounds us. Most of those negative thoughts will not even make contact with us, and those that do make it through our ear-gate or eye-gate will have no chance of surviving once they encounter the truth-based principle-thoughts with which we have already filled our minds and hearts.**

But if our *mental immune system* is weak, the negative thoughts will penetrate our minds and begin to incubate for future birth and plant seeds for a future harvest of multiplied doubts, fears, failures, and an overall pessimistic outlook of life.

We cannot always predict all the exact details of how we are going to get to the next higher level. The exact meetings, events, people and other factors that will aid us may not be clear to us beforehand. But even though we may not be able to see what will happen for months or years down the road, we can still have a strong, continual "Now-Knowing" that *all things are working together for our good.*

If we are shortsighted and take every thing that happens on a daily basis simply at face value, then we will miss much of our future good.

The spiritual law here: "And we know that all things work together for good to them that love God, to them that are the called according to His purpose."

Love God and say yes to His purpose for freedom in your life, and you are guaranteed that ALL things will work together for your good.

I love the first three words of this spiritual law--"And we know". No matter what the outer circumstances look like right now, you and I can still continue "flowing in our knowing!"

A few weeks ago I received an order from a person in Nigeria who contacted me through my Web site. This person from Africa placed an order for two hundred copies of my book "The Resilient Power Of Purpose".

It is not uncommon for orders of this quantity, or even orders for much larger quantities of my books, to be phoned or faxed in to my office. Usually people who want to order a large quantity of books will call or send an email through my Web site first to see what kind of special price or volume discount they will be able to get.

In hindsight, I should have noticed that this Nigerian order for two hundred books was a little strange because, first of all, the person who ordered the books bypassed the normal ordering process in the secure product section of my Web site and just clicked the "Contact Larry" button, which sent the email directly to me and not to my order department.

The second red flag I should have seen was that this person did not ask for any kind of discounted price and did not inquire as to how much the shipping cost would be from the U.S. to Nigeria. He just put the name and the address where the books were to be sent, gave the credit card number and expiration date, and said to ship the books via Express UPS or FedX and charge the cost of the books and shipping to the credit card. Of course another red flag was that the most expensive means of shipping had been selected. But I overlooked this red flag, mainly because I have had many orders for books within the U.S. and from many other countries around the world from people needing the books in a hurry to sell at some event only days away or from an organization that waited till the last minute to order my books for distribution to their "book of the month" club members. So I passed this order off as from just another person who had waited until the last minute to place the order, and I assumed that cost was not an issue but getting the books quickly was top priority.

Even though this person did not ask for a discounted price on the order of two hundred books, I did not feel right about charging the full retail price, so I instructed my office to give the normal discounted price on that quantity of books. We found out what the cost would be for the books to be shipped via UPS International Express, which is one of the fastest and most costly shipping methods available. My office then charged the total cost of the books, plus the shipping, to the credit card that was provided with the order. The charge of several thousand dollars went through fine, and we received a confirmation number that the charge was approved via the phone line into our credit card machine, which printed out on the receipt that the charge was accepted and the money would be credited to my business bank account.

There was a bit of a rush to get the books packed and to fill out all of the customs forms needed for an international shipment of this type, but I remember that my office did get the books shipped out to Nigeria that same day.

The next day I received a phone call from the security department of the merchant credit card company that processes the credit card transactions for my business. The gentleman who called asked, "Mr. DiAngi, do you know the individual who gave you the credit card number **** **** **** **** for a charge of several thousand dollars yesterday?" I said, "No, I do not know that person. He placed an order through my Web site." The man on the other end of the line said, "Well, I am sorry to have to inform you that that was a fraudulent charge. Do you have the name and address of the person who placed that order with your company?" I said, "Yes," and then gave him the name and address in Nigeria to which the books had been shipped. The security person informed me that the information I had just given to him did not match the credit card number and, in fact, the credit card with that number and expiration date actually belonged to someone with a completely different name who lived in the United States. The security person then told me that I needed to run a credit back to that card number immediately, returning the money back into the U.S. credit card holder's account to avoid a chargeback and some other problems that would eventually occur. So I had my office immediately run the credit back to the person who owned the card.

At first I thought, "Well, I guess I just got ripped off for several thousand dollars". I called UPS to see if they could stop the shipment of books, but they said that the books had already left the U.S. and were on a plane going to Germany, which was one of the distribution points that would forward the books to Nigeria. The customer service lady with UPS said, "Mr. DiAngi, at this point there is no way to stop the books from getting to Nigeria, but if you want to stop the delivery of this shipment, you have three options. You can have the boxes of books rerouted to another address in Nigeria, you can pay to have the books shipped back to you at a shipping cost of $903.00, or you can have the books abandoned, which means that the boxes of books will not be delivered and they will be destroyed."

I thought for a second, and my first reaction prompted this thought: "Well, I do not know anyone else in Nigeria to whom I could reroute the books, and I would rather have those books destroyed than to let this dishonest person who tried to rip me off have them." So I said to the lady, "I want to have the books abandoned." She said, "Okay, I will fax to you a form that you will need to sign and fax back to me in order for the shipment to be stopped. Once I receive your signature on the form, I will then contact the German distribution center to have them mark the boxes abandoned, and they will be destroyed".

Within a few minutes the fax from UPS arrived at my office. As I looked at the fax, I felt immediately convicted in my heart that to sign the form to have the books destroyed would be the wrong thing to do. I thought, "Wait a minute, I know that I am flowing in my purpose today, therefore there has to be a blessing hidden somewhere in this seemingly dark situation. What is the possible upside here? Well, there are two hundred books with a message of hope and purpose on their way to Nigeria. Even if this fraudulent person sells these books and makes a profit by selling them, two hundred people will receive a message of hope and purpose, and who knows how many lives will be changed for the better as a result of them having received these books."

So I called the UPS lady back and told her that I had changed my mind and I wanted the books to be delivered as previously scheduled. She said, "Okay, we will let the shipment go through, and it will be delivered on this coming Tuesday."

I told my wife, Julie, about the fraudulent book order and thought a few times later in that day about how I had been foolish to let someone take advantage of me like that. I then began to work on my thoughts to try to concentrate on the possibility that a few of those books might get into the hands and hearts of some people who really needed them in Nigeria.

At first, I will admit that I was a little "bummed out" and had some pretty strong feelings of resentment toward the individual who had placed that order. The name given me was a man's name, but since the credit card number was fraudulent, I figured that the name could have been a fake too. I will also admit that it was difficult to forgive this person who had played me for a fool, but I did forgive him or her, whoever they were, and I released them and prayed that they would possibly even be helped by reading my book!

It just so happened that the week after I received that fraudulent book order, I was traveling to South Africa and then on to Australia to speak ten times over the course of the following eighteen days.

When I got off the plane in South Africa that following Tuesday and was walking toward the baggage claim to collect my luggage, I checked my cell phone voice mail to see if I had missed any important calls while flying on an eight-hour flight to Amsterdam and another twelve-hour

hour flight from Amsterdam to Johannesburg. One of the voice mail messages was from the lady at UPS. She said they had attempted to deliver the packages to the person and address in Nigeria that my office had designated, but there was no person by that name to receive the boxes at that address! Then she closed her voice mail message with the question, "Do you want us to ship these boxes back to you, or do you want them abandoned and destroyed?" I thought, "Well I don't want to pay $903.00 to have the books shipped back to my office, so after all of this hassle, I guess the books will have to be destroyed."

When I received this phone message, it was about 9:00 AM in South Africa but 3:00 AM in the U.S., so I could not call the UPS service lady at that moment. I got pretty busy with the speaking engagements in South Africa and didn't get a chance to call UPS back until a couple of days later. I wasn't worried about it because I knew UPS would hold the packages until they heard from me.

I will confess that at the moment I got the news that the books would have to be destroyed, I once again had to deal with feelings of resentment toward that person who had placed the fraudulent order. My exact thoughts were, "That person must be a real jerk to take the time to place a fake order for these books and then not even be at the address he or she said to ship them to. This is absurd. What an evil person this individual must be." You talk about feeling that someone had rejected you...not only did I feel I had been rejected, I knew that someone went out of his or her way to rip me off. I wondered, "Was there a specific reason why this person picked me to commit this crime against, or does this person just do this type of thing for fun?"

Then I came back to my "right mind" and realized that it would not only do me harm and weigh me down if I held these ill feelings of bitterness towards this person, but it would also short circuit my attracting faith and cause my charisma to become contaminated.. Other people would sense this out-of-sync charisma, and it could sabotage the good that I was trying to manifest and could possibly also repel the people with whom I was talking that day. Holding unforgiveness is never a good idea. It only weakens us. In fact, the person we are holding the unforgiveness against could even possibly be hoping that we are feeling stressed out about what they did to us.

Once again, I had to release the feelings of rejection, unforgiveness, and resentment and obey the spiritual law which states "We must bless those who curse us". So I prayed that this person would be blessed. Then I forced myself to stop thinking about this person and worked to replace those thoughts with something more positive. I began thinking about truth-based principles and began preparing for the next presentations I would be sharing with the people in South Africa.

While in South Africa I spoke at a conference of about one thousand people. The leaders who had invited me to that conference were a husband and wife whose first names are Charlie and Alta. After I had finished my pre-sentation, I left the platform to go to the display table and started autographing my books and CD packs as people were buying them. After a couple of hours, I signed the final book for that evening and got up from the chair to go back to the hotel.

Just before I left, Charlie came over to the table, and we began talking with each other. During the course of that conversation, I mentioned in passing that I had received a fraudulent order of two hundred books through my Web site from someone in Nigeria.

Charlie immediately looked at me and said, "I have

over sixty thousand people who are distributors in my business organization in Nigeria. I'll buy those books from you. Here is my credit card. Just charge whatever the books cost to my card, and I will give you the name and address of one of my distributor leaders where you can have UPS reroute the book shipment to!" I thanked Charlie and thought "Wow, this is amazing!"

A few weeks after I had returned to the U.S., I received a phone call from Charlie, and he said the people in his Nigerian business organization loved my book and they would be ordering many more books from me. Then he gave me the names of the people who would be doing the ordering so that when I saw their names on the next Nigerian book order, I would know that it is real and not fraudulent.

Wow, what a miracle! Not only did two hundred people receive my book in Nigeria, but thousands more will do so in the future. Charlie also said that he has business conferences in Nigeria with over six thousand people in attendance and he will be talking to his leaders there about my coming to speak at one of those conferences!

This fraudulent Web site order that I originally thought was not only a rejection but a real slap in the face and at first glance left me feeling "ripped off and played for a fool" has now opened the door to reach thousands of people with this message of hope and purpose!

I remembered the story of "Joseph and his coat of many colors" when he faced his brothers who had tried to kill him and then sold him as a slave, which resulted in thirteen years of extreme adversity, hardship, and even false attempted rape charges that landed him in prison for a period of time. Then, when he finally went to the next higher level of his dream-purpose, the dream that he had thirteen years earlier came to pass, and he sat on a throne as a leader and ruler in charge of food distribution during a seven-year famine.

After thirteen years his brothers came to him and asked him for help to feed their family. Instead of taking revenge on his brothers for the adversity that they had assigned him to for over a decade, he said, "I am your brother Joseph, whom you sold into slavery." While I'm sure his brothers started "shaking in their boots," Joseph followed up with this amazing statement, "Fear not, for what you meant for evil, God meant for good."

Yes, we can know that ALL things are working together for our good even when it looks as though just the opposite is happening!

That situation, which I first thought was a huge rejection and a major violation against me from someone in Nigeria, has now "worked together for my good". What I first thought was "The Curse from Nigeria" has now become "The Blessing from Nigeria." Thank you, God, and thank you, Charlie! I believe that God wanted my books in Nigeria, and that God must have a sense of humor, because he made one of the Devil's servants place the order on my Web site!!

As you flow in your purpose, similar things will happen to you. What at first seems to be a curse will turn into an amazing positive breakthrough. As we keep our thoughts right and stay purpose-driven on a daily basis, we will be like the cream that always rises to the top. Not only will the people who reject us never have the power to slow us down or stop us, but, without even realizing it, they can help us by *rejecting us forward*!

Chapter
7

Exude an Attracting Charisma

Why is it that some people have a positive magnetic quality about them to the extent that all they have to do is walk into a room and say a few words, and all of the positive people in the room are drawn to them? While I am asking this question I guess it only makes sense to also examine the other side of the coin and pose this next question as well. Why is it that other people seem to attract negative or even abusive people and have a repelling quality about them that seems to cause positive people to want to run in the opposite direction after only a few seconds of conversation? Physical beauty is not the main factor in this attracting or repelling quality. IQ is not the main factor. Being dressed in the most up-to-date fashion is not the main factor. While these and many other physically or mentally desirable features of one's self do play a part in either attracting or repelling people, these alone are only accessories. I believe it is safe for me to say that we have all met some physically attractive, well dressed people who appear to have an above average intellect who did not impress us to be someone with whom we really wanted to become close friends.

There is something that is not well detected by our physical five senses and even surpasses the power of intellect. This quality that makes the greatest impact on the people we meet is our charisma. Charisma is exuded and received at our heart-level. At every moment of every day you and I are either exuding an attractive charisma or a repelling charisma. Just as we cannot see the wind but we can very clearly see the effects of the wind all around us, charisma has this same invisible reality about it. The kind of charisma we are exuding determines whether people feel safe in our presence or feel unsure about our intentions. It is a huge factor in whether people believe that we are being real or if we are "faking it" and whether they should be confident about us or be skeptical. All of our words and actions are seasoned with the kind of charisma that we are exuding.

In specific context with building a vision, mission, or business where we are asking people to join with us in the pursuit of freedom, there is something we can deliberately do to make sure that we are exuding the right kind of positive, attracting charisma at all times. This "something" that we can deliberately do is what I call "stepping over the line and going beyond the point of no return."

Here is another seed that we planted earlier, and now we're going to water it a little bit. If you have read any of my other books or attended my live speeches or workshops, you may have heard me talk about the principle of "stepping over the line and going beyond the point of no return". In my six CD program "OWN YOUR DREAM, The Resilient Power Of Purpose" I teach how to daily stay "stepped over the line" by practicing a program of "thought-replacement and thought-exchange." The principles in this program are first to be applied on a personal level, and then I show you how to work thought-replacement and thought-exchange to build a strong vision or business. In my twelve CD teaching program, "BREAKTHROUGH LEADERSHIP," I teach how to "stay stepped over the line" and practice thought-replacement and thought-exchange on a leadership level.

I explain and show how to work with principles that will help any individual to build stronger personal confidence as a leader, and then I give you methods you can use to help the people that you are leading to get past their fears, insecurities, feelings of unworthiness, etc.

In the next few paragraphs I am going to illustrate how this foundational principle of "stepping over the line" will directly help you to be resilient enough to overcome rejection and to keep applying the layering approach that I have explained earlier in this book.

The layering approach is something many people fail to follow through on successfully because they are too impatient and want instant gratification. Many people will ask for something just once, and if they don't get it immediately, they quit and move on to something that will be easier for them to accomplish. But to build a great vision, mission, or business we must be resilient enough to talk to the same people over and over again and ask the same questions over and over again to apply the necessary amount of layers. After a period of time we will reach a place of mutual respect and establish a strong enough connection with some of these individuals to see a breakthrough take place.

Resiliency is a vital quality that you must possess in order to keep calling people over and over again and to keep applying one layer after another without becoming discouraged. Most people become discouraged if they talk to a person two or three times and haven't yet achieved their desired results. If you want to accomplish great things, getting discouraged after two or three phone calls won't "cut it." Only average and mediocre results can be born out of this type of approach. Many human beings are working a job that they dislike or even hate in order to make money. If they dislike or hate that job, then why do they keep on working there for twenty or forty years? One reason is that they believe the only way they will be able to make it in life is if they work for someone else. Whoever that "someone else" is that they are working for is probably a person or group of people who built that business and continue to build that business by making lots of phone calls, meeting with lots of people, and calling some of them over and over again to negotiate and get more business. As a result of this proactive strategy their employees will continue to have more work to complete on the assembly line or on whatever kind of work is necessary to make the products or deliver the service that they are in business to supply.

Those who are not willing to make the phone calls and meet with people to build their own vision or business will end up working for someone else who is willing to *talk to the many to find the few*...Instead of making their own dreams become a reality, they spend their whole lives working at a job they dislike so that they can make their bosses dreams become a reality!

If we want to achieve greatness and build <u>our own</u> great vision, mission, or business, we will need to make some quality decisions *upfront*. **We must be willing to do all of the things that others are not willing to do, if we want to have the success that others will never have.**

Someone once said, "Success is a decision." Yes, it starts with one decision and then it is continued with the daily consistency of following through on the initial decision that we made.

There is *a line,* that each of us either decide to step over and go beyond or we decide to avoid this line and live our lives in some form of comfort zone as an alternative existence.

I call this dividing line "The Point of No Return." Stepping over the line and going beyond the point of no return will determine the specific type of charisma that we are exuding on a daily, hour by hour, and minute by minute basis.

As a ship crosses the ocean, it comes to a point where it has used up too much fuel and can no longer turn around and go back to its' origin. It must now go on to its' destination. As a plane taxies down the runway, it gets to a point where it has built up too much thrust and lift, and it has used up too much of the runway so that it cannot abort its mission. It must take off and fly.

Certainly once those wheels lift off the ground and the plane has left the airport, the decision of whether or not to take off is no longer a consideration. It is now the "real deal." That plane better fly or else…. The pilot can't put that plane in reverse and fly backwards to get back on the ground. It has to continue flying forward, and that is that!

Whichever side of the line we are operating from will determine the kind of charisma we are exuding, and the kind of charisma we are exuding will determine whether people will be attracted to us or will be repelled away from us.

Stepping over the line is simply the act of making a 100% commitment to your vision and your purpose.

At this point someone may ask, "How do I know whether I am on the right side or the wrong side of the line?"

Remember, the difference is that on the wrong side of the line, before you have made the quality decision to *go beyond the point of no return*, the option to quit still exists for you.

Before we step over that line we can still buy the concept of giving up, turning back and quitting. If things get tough, if enough people disappoint us, if we run into financial challenges or adversity, etc., we can still leave a route of escape open so that we can bail out. And we can spend the rest of our lives taxiing around the airport, pretending that we are an eagle instead of a chicken!!

But **once you have stepped over that line, quitting is no longer an option**. Quitting is nowhere to be found--not in your head, not in your heart, not in the words that you speak...nowhere...it is nowhere in your being. Someone talking to you about quitting would be like having someone trying to convince you to put your hand into a meat grinder...No Way!!!!

So what does this have to do with overcoming rejection? It really has everything to do with it. In fact, if we have not "stepped over the line" and made a 100% commitment, we are actually setting ourselves up to be a magnet that will attract rejection!

Which side of the line we are on determines the kind of charisma we are exuding, and the kind of charisma we are exuding at any one given moment has the greatest effect on the person we are communicating with, even a stronger effect than the actual audible words we are speaking.

If we can explain our vision, mission, or business opportunity with perfect oratory and flawless linguistics but our charisma is weak and insecure because we are on the wrong side of the line, *where quitting is still an option*, then no matter how convincing our audible words may be, there is a good possibility that the person listening to us is going to back off and find some kind of excuse not to say yes to the proposed opportunity.

Why? Because, as I have just mentioned, all of our words and actions are flavored and seasoned with the particular type of charisma that we are exuding at a *heart level* at any given moment.

As a person talks, underneath the audible words they are speaking, there is always another kind of communication occurring. Simultaneously there is the transmission of an inaudible charisma that exudes from the *heart level* of the one speaking and hits the person who is listening at their *heart level*. A person can learn how to fake a lot of things in life. An individual can learn to talk a little slicker, can learn to ask leading and tie-down closed-ended questions to try to manipulate people. There are a lot of techniques we can learn to use on a superficial level when we are operating strictly from our outer self. But heart level charisma cannot be faked. It is what it is. We either have a "wrong side of the line charisma" or a "right side off the line charisma" exuding from us, every moment of every day.

If quitting and giving up is still an option for us personally, then it doesn't matter how convincing our audible words are. The charisma exuding from us at a heart level is communicating *the truth* loud and clear. No matter how confident our words may seem to be, people listening to us can still feel *the truth*--that our commitment level does not match our words. They receive the transmission of our weak charisma, which reveals to them that we could quit and give up at any given moment.

We have all had the experience of someone trying to sell us something--or maybe our son or daughter was trying to explain where he or she was last night-- and after we listened to this person talking to us, the only way to describe what we were picking up on a charisma level would be to say, "It all sounded good, but it just didn't feel right." This is an example of a situation in which the words that someone is speaking do not match the charisma he or she is exuding. So, as we communicate with another person, if the words that we speak are "right on" but our charisma is "off center," then most likely we will not receive the reaction we want from that person, and unknowingly we may even be causing them to reject us!

On the other hand, it is a fact that even if we do not possess the best communication skills but are 100% committed and have *gone beyond the point of no return--where quitting is no longer an option*--people will still be attracted to us like a magnet and will want to join us simply because the charisma that they sense from us is rock solid.

In fact, it is often the case that even when the person listening doesn't totally understand the full picture of the plan we are proposing, they will sometimes still decide to join us because of the confident, committed charisma we are transmitting.

The reason for this is that the charisma we, as "100% committed people," are exuding speaks a loud and clear message at a heart level: *"Friend, this vision that I am explaining to you is the "real deal" and I am in this thing for the long haul. I am not going to quit no matter what. If you join me in this pursuit, you will never have to wonder about my commitment to you and to your success. I will be your greatest booster. Together we will do whatever it takes to go from one level of freedom to another higher level, and nothing will stop us. We will laugh together, cry together, we will go through days when everything is going great, and we will also go through days when things seem to be going all wrong. And even if in the process of getting to our next higher level we fall on our face, we are still going to make sure that at least we fall forward, because then we will still know that we have gotten five to six feet closer to our dreams. If we don't have the answers, then we will find a leader on a higher level who does have the answers, and we are going to figure this thing out one step at a time. I am with you 100% plus...all the way and we are not going to stop until we have achieved total freedom in every area of our lives."*

If this is the kind of inaudible message being transmitted via your heart level charisma while you are talking, you will have many people say, "Yes, where do I sign up to join you in this thing?" And often those people may not even fully know why they want to join with you! They just know that you are a person they can trust. They feel safe in your presence, and they know you are the kind of person they want to be with.

Here is a leadership shift point: *Most people will not join us in any vision, mission, or business at the very beginning because they actually believe that they are going to be a success in whatever we are proposing to them. Also, most people, when they first say yes to us, still will not necessarily believe that our specific opportunity or proposal will actually work for them!* They may believe that it will work for you, for me, or for others who have proven it to work, but for the most part the average person won't believe that any new idea is necessarily going to work for them personally. In fact, most people's self esteem has been so beat up and damaged throughout their lives, that by the time we get to them with any new idea or opportunity, they really are not in good enough shape mentally or emotionally to believe that they can become a success at much of anything.

When people first agree to join with you and say, "Yes, sign me up" and "I want to go forward," most of the time they have said yes for one main reason...*because of the way you helped them to feel better about themselves while they were in your presence*. The bottom line in their final decision to say "Yes" was because of a thought that was created in their mind and heart as they were exposed to your "right side of the line" charisma. In their minds and hearts a desire was birthed that created this type of a thought, "It really feels good to be with this person, and I want some more of this good feeling."

No, they don't actually know that they will be a success yet, but they do know one thing for sure--when they are in your presence, they always feel better about themselves, and somewhere in the background they may also have a hope that your proposal to bring freedom in their lives may actually be possible for them too.

People may enjoy being around their families for many reasons, but when it comes to the subject of financial freedom, it may be depressing because their family situation tells them that there is no way to get ahead financially, especially if they are in extreme debt.

Work for people may be oppressing, because the strategy and intention of many employers and management is to keep the employees feeling small and off balance. Employers often like to keep their people feeling like they have been done the biggest favor in the world by being allowed to have their job, and if they don't measure up to the company standards and expectations, they can be fired and replaced within a few minutes with any one of a thousand other people who are waiting to take their job. This method of propaganda that many employers and management use is deliberately targeted at keeping total control over the people working for them. They do not like people to feel too good about themselves, because if the worker does feel too confident they might wake up to the fact that they deserve much more than what that particular job has to offer.

So in the context of making money and having financial freedom, many people get depressed when they are with their families, and they may be oppressed at their jobs. But then when they get around you, they feel that maybe there is hope for some greater possibilities for the future. Here's a good question to ask yourself: "If they are oppressed at their job and depressed when they are with their friends and family, but when they get around you they feel hope, who are they going to want to keep spending more and more time with? The answer is obvious. "IT'S YOU."

A magical moment

The magic happens when the people we have been communicating with have had enough exposure to our positive charisma for them to reach critical mass in their decision-making process. For some people it will be the third time or the twentieth time or maybe not until the forty-third time. It will take a different number of exposures for different people. But during one of those times when they are in your presence, as you are consistently exuding the right kind of charisma, they will reach critical mass, and guess what will happen? Yep, that's right, the individuals you have been purposed to work with will *step over the line*, and they will *go beyond the point of no return*, and now you really have some great people to work with. Each person that steps over that line is an individual that you can help to develop into a great leader. But what caused most of those people to keep coming back to be with you over and over again until they had a shift in their thinking and they chose to *step over that line*? It was simply because you are a person whom it feels good to be around. They kept coming back to you to get that good, hopeful, faith-filled feeling enough times until they could have faith for their own success and see themselves as worthy of going to their next higher level.

One of the greatest, most powerful things that ever occur on this earth is when one person believes in another person, even before that other person believes in himself or herself. Thank God for great mentors who see what is possible for us and keep working with us until we can see those possibilities as our own.

Chapter

8

Talk to Many to Find the Few Who Will Find the Many

I referred to this principle in passing in an earlier chapter. It is such an important truth that it is vital we go into more depth and take a closer look at how this law of "Talking to many to find the few" works in everyday life and business. As you have probably noticed by now, part of my style in teaching is that I will plant the seed of a principle, then later come back to water and fertilize that seed to help it grow. Well, that's what we are doing here with this law-based principle. If you will talk to "the many" to find "the few that you are meant to work with", then "the few" that you find will go out to find "the many". But first you must pay the price to "Talk to the many".

Great leaders are people who have made a 100% commitment to their vision, purpose, and mission. Whether people appear to be accepting them or rejecting them at any given moment does not have much effect on their level of confidence and passion for what they believe in the depths of their hearts and what they know to be true.

Great leaders know it is a simple fact of reality and always will be that there are different kinds of people who will always react in different ways to the same exact idea or opportunity. Great leaders do not question their own validity when people react in different ways to them. Great leaders understand that these "different reactions" are usually an issue that has to do with the "mind set" of the person doing the reacting.

In fact, great leaders who have worked with many people over the years have come to an understanding that the way in which different kinds of people will react to an idea or an opportunity when it is presented to them is actually quite predictable. People who are unhappy with their lives will often respond with a certain degree of pessimism... People who love life and are positive about themselves and their family often react in the opposite way.

People who were raised in a family where their parents owned their own business can often easily grasp the idea of becoming an independent business owner, whereas people who were raised in a family where everyone has always worked for a company owned by someone else often have a bit more of a challenge in making the mental leap toward believing that they can actually be successful at building their own independent business.

As I mentioned earlier, many people's self-esteem has been so beat up over the years that they have a self-esteem deficit, and they have to look up, just to see the bottom! So by the time you or I get to them with an idea that they could use to improve their life, they are at such a low belief level that when we first propose a new idea to them, they can't see themselves being a real success at much of anything.

The amazing thing is that as we work with some of these people who have a low self-esteem, and as we help them gain a larger vision of themselves and the greater possibilities for their lives, they can become superstars who break all the records and accomplish the most tremendous things.

It is a good idea to remind yourself every morning, before you start your day, to consciously make a decision to look at each individual that you encounter as the person he or she could become if provided with high quality mentoring.

In daily life, as we rush through each twenty-four hours, we can tend to forget some of the most important truth principles. Even though we make the phone calls, meet with people, and do the work to build our vision, we can possibly self-sabotage the work that we do if we do not consciously live with the continual awareness of this leadership principle, **"visualize people as who they can become rather than who they appear to be during our first encounter with them"**

To be able to look beneath the surface and to see the inward potential of a person, we must be leaders who operate with strong faith, and to operate with strong faith requires that we meditate on a higher level of thoughts than that of the *common thinking* masses of people. To be able to hold a vision that goes beyond the superficial, we must have the faith to know that every person was created to manifest greatness. The most obvious potential that a person reveals to us is usually only the tip of the iceberg. To have this kind of faith to see the potential that is not first obvious will require that we feed our faith every day.

There is a guarantee in Psalms chapter one that if "one's delight is in the law" (in the truth) and "in the law doth he or she meditate day and night...whatsoever she or he does will prosper" This ability to "see people as who they can become, rather than who they first appear to be" requires a daily and continuous repetition, review, and reinforcement on our part by "meditating on the truth". As we spend each day and night meditating on truth-based principles, we will develop an intuitive sense of what is true and what is not true. This is very important, because this world is filled with half-truths, deceptions, and lies that have been accepted by the masses as the absolute truth. If we want to find out the truth about another human being, we will always have to use our intuitive sense to see who that person really is, rather than become overly influenced by outward appearances.

A truly savvy leader is always looking for the gold that is hidden in the individual they are working and communicating with. Just as it is possible that you or I could meet a person who is dressed in jeans and an average shirt and not realize that he or she is in actuality someone who has a net worth of one hundred million dollars, it is also possible that you or I could meet someone who does not immediately outwardly show that she or he has a great desire to learn, grow and be successful. The tip of an iceberg can be only a few percent of the total mass that exists beneath the surface of the water. And so it is with what is first visible about most people.

There is a spiritually based foundational principle that admonishes us to "judge not according to the outward appearances." I will be the first to admit that to stay in a "knowing place" in connection with this leadership truth-based principle, it takes a lot of meditating, reading, being taught by a strong mentor, listening to uplifting music, and continually receiving inspiration and truth from many different sources.

Yes, there are some people who do not seem to have all of the outward indicators of success, yet they do have a deep hunger to go to their next higher level in life. While we invest our time and energy in helping some of these people we may have to help them get unstuck and help them to overcome insecurities, feelings of unworthiness, fears and doubts. It is not always easy to help a person to build their faith until they can see the right picture of the confident and successful person that they can become. But if we have a truly compassionate leader's heart, we will remember the time in our lives when we needed a mentor to believe in us before we could believe in ourselves.

We have also looked at the following leadership principle in a briefer fashion a few paragraphs ago, but now let's "water and fertilize" this truth and take a look at this principle from another angle. *At the very beginning, when people say yes to you, at the very first moment that a person agrees to join you in whatever vision, mission, or opportunity that you are presenting, most people will not be joining you because they actually believe that they can be successful or because they actually believe that what you are proposing will work for them.*

Remember this fact: The main reason why many people will first decide to join with you is simply because of the way you helped them to feel about themselves when they were in your presence. Their desire to join and become a part of your vision was born out of the reality that they felt better when they were with you than when they were with other people!'

Ok, let's take a closer look at the kind of people that we are looking for. In building any vision, mission, or business, we are looking for people who will allow us to help them make a shift to a larger vision for their lives. Any person can make the shift from unhappy to happy or from not believing that they could own their own business to believing that they could. In fact, people switch from positive to negative and from the negative to the positive every day. The possibility for change is available to everyone, but everybody will not necessarily want to change to the positive or see themselves as the kind of person who can take a leap to their next higher level. Some will and some won't. So, **to be a great leader, we must also be a great talent scout**. One of the greatest qualities that a person can possess is a *willingness to learn*. We must always be on the *look out* for people who are <u>teachable</u> and <u>willing</u> to <u>allow</u> us to mentor them. When we have the choice to mentor a person who appears to have less experience and less outward talent but is very willing and teachable vs. the choice to work with a person who seems to have more experience and more outward talent but is resistant to receiving our teaching and training, it is always the wiser choice to work with the person with a teachable and willing spirit. It is much easier and much less stressful to help an individual gain more experience and increase her or his level of talent than to pour our time and effort into a seemingly more talented person who is going to resist our efforts to help them.

Because we all have only a limited about of time and energy to invest in people, sometimes we have to also choose between working with a person who has proven to be loyal to us and trying to mentor a person who seems to have more outward advantages but has questionable loyalty. In this case it is always better to invest our time and energy in the person with the highest level of loyalty. A lack of loyalty is a deep character flaw that is very difficult to correct. A person with a lack of loyalty and integrity will sooner or later end up "biting you in the behind" every time!

Every person is different and has spent a lifetime feeding on a primary diet of either positive or negative thoughts in order to become the kind of person that he or she is at the moment we first meet them. Great leaders understand this fact very clearly. Therefore they know that if they talk with ten different people they are probably going to get ten different unique reactions. Even if there are only subtle differences from one person to another, a great leader knows how to distinguish the smallest differences in a specific person's personality and the slightest signs of strength, weakness, security, insecurity, nervousness, peace, belief, doubt, truthfulness, dishonesty, and so forth.

Since great leaders are aware of these differences from one person to the next, they no longer take it personally when someone seems to be rejecting them. A great leader knows that the way a person reacts is simply the predictable way that that type of person always reacts to an idea or possibility of the type being proposed.

We can't do anything about *where people are at* in their minds and hearts when we first find them. But if they will allow us to, we can help them to change their thinking so that they can go to a higher level of freedom spiritually, in relationships, mentally, emotionally, financially, and in every other area of life.

A savvy leader knows that there are certain people who can immediately see the "big picture," and then there are some other people who can't see it if you press the picture up against their nose. Great leaders understand that **the only people who are going to closely relate to a larger vision are the individuals who have allowed life to prepare them for something bigger and better than their present circumstances.** Some people get "better" and some people get "bitter," and great leaders know that the bitter people are probably going to also be the "no" people. Great leaders see this as "just fine" because they don't really need a bitter person on their team anyway!

If we keep our hearts and our minds in the right place, filled with the truth about who God created us to be and the great purpose that we were placed on earth to fulfill, then we don't need or look for other people to validate our self worth. As we stay free from needing others to validate us, we are also free from the possibility of being emotionally injured when people don't react positively to us or our ideas.

The more we keep ourselves focused on purpose, the less of an effect the "small thinking" people will have on us.

I am sure that if you have been in a leadership position for very long at all, you have presented an opportunity to people and laid out a system for them that you know will work for them "if they work it." I am also sure that as you did this, there have been certain people who have looked back at you and acted as if you were speaking in a language that is totally foreign to them. Some people do not want a plan that will require them to take consistent action on a daily basis. Even if the steps you are sharing with them are very simple, some folks are always looking for the "easy way" to success. Well, you and I both know that there is no easy way to success. I do not mean to be unkind when I say this, but the plain truth is that some people are lazy, and they think they are entitled to special privileges without working for them or paying any kind of price to manifest a better life. The "lottery" mentality has done much damage to people's perception over the years. People see a billboard along side the road that advertises that if they buy a state lottery ticket, they could win a hundred million dollars, and somehow they think that they are entitled to that money! They go to the corner store and buy a ticket for a few dollars and hope that later that same day, while sitting in their favorite comfortable chair watching the evening news on TV, they'll find out that they have picked the winning lottery number and are now a hundred million dollars richer. They actually believe that, because they spent one, two, or five dollars on a lottery ticket, they deserve to be rewarded with millions of dollars! The thought of working a plan every day to build wealth is repulsive to them. It is also amazing that many people who will spend ten or even fifty dollars at one time for lottery tickets would never think of spending that same amount of money to buy books or CD teaching programs to improve their lives!

The truth is that many people will spend forty or fifty hours a week working at a job they hate and will complain that they are not making enough money, but they are not willing to even work ten hours a week in an endeavor that will build financial freedom for them and their family. Again, I do not mean to be unkind when I say this, but these are not the kind of people that I want to be working on my team or with me to build a vision or a business.

So as we are proposing an opportunity for success to people, we must realize that sometimes a reaction that may appear to be a rejection from a person may actually be a result of the fact that they were hoping we were going to help them find the "Yellow Brick Road" that will lead them to the Wizard who will magically and instantly make their dreams come true. This type of person will become disappointed when, instead of offering them the "Yellow Brick Road," we present to them a vision or a business that they could get passionate enough about to work day and night to give birth to success. They would have preferred that we would have given them a quick "magic pill" that would grant to them a fantasy dream life of wealth and privilege.

This "get something for nothing" mentality clouds people's minds and distorts their thinking. Even though it seems crazy, it is possible that as you are proposing an idea or an opportunity to people who have a distorted way of thinking about success, they may instantly think that they are more of an expert than you are on what you are talking about. You may know that the system and the plan you are proposing to them has worked for you and for hundreds of other people who have gone before you and has produced great results and great success. Yet even though you know these people are not grasping the value and importance of the steps you are laying out for them, it is amazing to find that for some reason they think they have a system that will work even better than yours, and they will not let go of the fallacy that they know more than you do!

Sometimes the only thing that you can do with people like this is to let them go off by themselves and try "their system" on their own so they do not infect the other people in your group. It is often not long before they either disappear all together or they come back to you with their tail between their legs and very humbly say something like this: "Could you please explain your business system to me one more time? I think I may have missed something the first time, and the system I tried didn't work very well." Now they are finally teachable and ready to learn.

Building a network with a strong leadership foundation

Building a network of people who will work with you with a focused vision in any pursuit is very important. Alone, we can accomplish only a limited amount. For example, if you want to build a small business, you can build a business that depends completely on your own individual efforts, and you can enjoy having a small business with a limited income. But *if you want to build a huge business, then you will have to develop leaders* who will *work with you in a collaborative effort*. This is a law of success that cannot be circumvented. As we develop strong leaders, they will become the front-line people who will join with us in building a vision, mission, pursuit, or business.

Of the many people who will come and go as we move forward, we must be able to discern which individuals we should spend more of our time working with and which people we should spend a less amount of our mentoring time with. It would be nice if everyone who decided to join with us would become 100% committed to the vision and really start to make things happen, but in truth the "100% committed people" are a rare breed indeed. It is very liberating to constantly be aware of the truth that *most people are not at a place in life where they can believe that they can be a success.* We may desire that everyone we meet will be prepared and ready for greater blessings in their lives, but without fertile ground the seeds of blessing that we offer to them may not be able to take root and grow. For this reason we must be careful to not become discouraged when we find that many of the people who initially join us will not be able to follow through with the commitments they make to us.

I mentioned the following principle-based law earlier in a different context, but now let's take a closer look at this law in the context of building a network of leaders. In building any vision where we are enrolling people to join us, **we must talk to the many to find the few.** By talking to *the many* to find *the few,* I believe we are simply in a "sorting process." **We are sorting through a lot of people to find the few that we were meant to be with all along. In fact, I believe that from a "destiny perspective"** *we are looking for the people who even before we were formed in our mother's womb and before they were formed in their mother's womb* **we were predestined and purposed to find them, and they were purposed to find us so that we could work together in a united cause and vision.**

Now, I must admit that I do not always like this "you must talk to many to find the few" law. I wish I could find "the few" without talking to "the many." I would rather that the next ten most significant people in my life and business would just call me on the phone, and we could meet in a restaurant at a table that seats eleven and begin to discuss all of the great things that we plan to do and the great dreams that we are going to make into a reality.

But the truth is that it is not going to be that easy. I may need to dial the phone a thousand times, leave a lot of voice mail messages and have many, many meetings before I find the next ten most significant people in my life and business.

It really doesn't matter if you or I like the "you must talk to the many to find the few" law. It is still the way success works when we are looking to attract other people to join us in our vision, mission, or business...and it will work to the extent that we work it!

Again, a wonderful thing to remember about this law is that if you work with it long enough, you will find that after you have talked to enough people to *find the few*, "the few" that you have found will then proceed to go out and find "the many"!

As we are determining and discerning which people we will invest more of our time to work with and more of our effort to help develop into strong leaders, it is also true that even after some people achieve a position of leadership, there is still a possibility that we could feel rejection from them. They may be all enthused at the beginning but then start to either put up their defenses or start to back away from us once they see the commitment and the work that will be necessary to go to the next higher level of building the vision.

It helps to know how to categorize people so that we deal with each individual in a way that is most effective in context with his or her thought and belief system. As we recognize where different people are at in their level of commitment to the collective vision, we can clearly see who deserves most of our personal mentoring.

The same principle that applies in a more general sense when we are first proposing a vision or opportunity to a person is even more important from a standpoint of developing strong leaders. In order to maintain the mental and emotional strength to nurture those who will be the "cream that rises to the top" in leadership, the wisest thing to do is to *work with the willing* and to not let the *unwilling* people drain us of our energy. The people who stay ready and willing will be a constant source of encouragement to you even in the toughest of times.

Chapter

9

Learn to Identify the Five Different Kinds of People

As we share ideas, our vision, our mission, or a business opportunity with others, the individuals who say yes to us and agree to join us will fall into on of five different categories:

1. <u>Unteachable People</u>

These are people who either refuse to be taught or are unable to receive our guidance and mentoring. The list of reasons why different individuals become *unteachable people* is almost endless. It could be that because of their insecurities, they cannot make themselves vulnerable to anyone, and therefore they fear that by opening themselves to receive teaching they may also expose what they perceive to be their personal flaws or weaknesses. It could be that they have been hurt by others who have manipulated or mistreated them, and they have developed a hard protective shell around themselves that is impenetrable. It could also be that they have not yet come to a place where they are humble enough to allow someone to teach them. People who have been somewhat successful in other areas of life may think they already "know it all" and do not realize that to start something new, they will need to be open to a new approach or strategy. The kind of families that people grow up in can also cause them to be unteachable.

People who were raised in families where they were taught by example to be skeptical about everything and everyone can have much difficulty trusting someone who is attempting to mentor them.

Of course all of these reasons, and many more that we could list here, come as a result of one type of insecurity or another, and at times there is no simple, quick way to help a person become teachable. We can allow these unteachable people to be a part of our group activities or meetings as long as they do not start to infect others with their unteachable attitude.

Often unteachable people won't hang around long enough to cause any real problems. I have found that many unteachable people will fairly quickly fade off into the distance and disappear because they start to feel a little out of place when they are around open-minded, teachable folks. As long as these people remain unteachable, it is not wise for us to give to them very much of our one-on-one mentoring time. If you are paying unteachable people a salary or hourly wage, it is obviously a good idea to dismiss them from their positions as soon as possible. If their compensation or rewards are all based on their production and you don't have to pay or reward them unless they produce results, then at times it is a good idea to let them hang around for you to see how they develop. If you ever start to see that they are having a negative effect on other people in the group, you will need to "care-front" them. With a non-emotional approach you can let them know that they are having a negative effect on others, and if they do not want to work in unity with the vision or business that you are building, then it would be in their best interest and yours if they would go find another group or business that they feel more suited for.

We could go on and on here about unteachable people,

but I don't think it is necessary to do so. Before we move on to the next type of person I must emphasize here that just because a person starts out with you in the "unteachable" category does not mean they will always be unteachable. It is not uncommon for an unteachable person to have a shift take place, which causes the individual to gradually or even suddenly become very teachable. For example: If you are helping people develop a business opportunity in the evenings, and they work a J.O.B. (Just Over Broke) during the day, if they should happen to lose their daytime J.O.B. and suddenly find themselves without income, they could become teachable very quickly. They can develop a sincere desire to learn the fastest way to excel in the opportunity that you have given to them when they are faced with the fact that their survival depends upon getting it going and at the fastest pace possible. Almost instantly, people faced with this type of "wake up call" in life can become very humble, ready to be taught, and able to move forward taking massive action.

2. <u>Rollercoaster People</u>

I'm sure that you have a good idea of what the *rollercoaster people* are like. As we continue to operate in a leadership position, we will see a lot of this type of people. They are up, excited, and ready to go one minute, and the next minute or the next day they are down in the dumps and depressed, with their lips dragging on the curb because they feel so low and discouraged. They are the "start and stop" and "start and stop again" people. We can help a lot of these folks get their plane up in the air and keep it up there if they are humble enough and teachable enough to let us do so. A rollercoaster person will either even out and then start to fly at an altitude somewhere above the curb, above the trees, or maybe even above the mountains, or they may crash and burn out, possibly to never be heard from again.

To a great extent our ability to help rollercoaster people depends on if we can help them start to dream bigger and be purpose-driven enough to overcome their tendency to continuously lose momentum. An "up and down" and "start and stop" existence is very exhausting, so is vitally important for us to help them eliminate this pattern of operation in their life and business. These people often have difficulty staying focused on "why" they are doing the work that is necessary to accomplish "what" they want to achieve. Therefore, it is important that we not only help them to find the five most important reasons of <u>why</u> they <u>must</u> get to their next higher level, but we will also need to check with them regularly to make sure that they are still focused on their Top Five. If we can help them find some personal, family, financial, achievement, recognition, or professional reasons and goals that are vitally important to them and if we can help them get their focus onto their purpose and off of their problems, it is amazing to see how this one adjustment in their perspective can cause them to take off like a rocket. If they will let us help them, people who start out as "rollercoaster people" can become real "go-getters."

3. <u>Incubator People</u>

Incubator people can be a bit difficult to figure out. Initially they say "yes," and they have enough vision to see the possibilities, which prompts them to want to join us in the pursuit of a higher level in life or business, but then they seem to go into a coma! You almost want to put your finger on their wrist to see if they still have a pulse or put a mirror under their nose to see if they are still breathing. They are like an egg that is just not ready to hatch yet. These folks are often sitting in the last row at meetings, and when you look at their activity level, you may even wonder why they ever bothered to show up at the meeting! At the beginning there is usually no way of knowing for sure what any of these "incubator people" will or will not become. They could finally hatch and become the lead runners in the pack, or they could just sit there until they dwindle away to nothing. Our responsibility as a leader is not to try to force them to hatch. Just as a mother eagle sits on her eggs and gives each egg the right environment to incubate in, we should also allow these incubator people the opportunity to hatch in the warmth of our vision, our commitment, our belief, and our positive, attractive charisma.

Again I must say that one of the most interesting things about "incubators" is that most of the time it is impossible to correctly prejudge what they will become. Our world is filled with stories of people who had an incubation period of weeks, months, or even years, but once they hatched they became some of the greatest superstars of all time!

4. Walkers

Walkers are the slow and steady people. They sign up for the vision and commit themselves to their purpose, and then every day they do a little bit to move forward.

If you look at the quantity of results they produce in one day, it may not seem very impressive. But if you look at the volume of results they have produced over a period of one month, six months, or a year, it really starts to add up to something that is making a noticeable positive difference and can even become quite substantial. Some people may never get all that fired up about breaking the records or being the number one achiever, but make no mistake about it; these slow and steady people can be powerful if they keep going for a long enough period of time. Every day they are creating a little additional momentum, and over a period of months and years they can be like the little stream of water that over time cuts its way through an entire mountain and becomes a roaring river. One of the reasons these walkers can produce a "roaring river" of results is because the cumulative-collective, compounding momentum that they create can cause them to attract people to join them who in turn become some of the biggest producers in your organization. Another reason why a consistent, steady "walker" can become very powerful is that, at first, every day's production works in addition to the previous day's activity, but when they have built a strong enough base to work from, their efforts no longer just result in addition, but the wide base that they have built over time causes them to shift from addition-momentum to multiplication-momentum! The pyramids were built by teams of people who worked together to cut and put in place a number of stones each day, and now they dominate the skyline in Egypt for miles in any direction. As steady walkers move forward in their consistent, persistent fashion, they can also lead you to some other people who are amazing go-getters, people who have the posture and charisma to become team leaders. Of course we know it is true that as we build any vision or business, there is growth that initially comes from the people we know or meet personally, but often the greatest growth comes from the people that they know or meet, and the people that the second line of people know or meet leads us to others who even outshine the first two people. These "walker" type people are a major factor in making a strong foundation in whatever vision you are building.

It's often not the people who can do the hundred-yard dash that make the biggest difference. A lot of people who run the hundred-yard dash in record time just end up fizzling out during the long haul. It is the people with continual Daily Consistency in keeping their thoughts positive and who are taking continual action that make the biggest difference over time.

5. Runners

Runners are most definitely a rare breed. They sign up with the vision, and then all you see is a trail of dust, fire, and smoke. They move with a tremendous sense of urgency and create big results fast. It might be a little humbling for us to admit, but the truth about some of these runners is that they would have become massively successful with or without our help and with or without our leadership. These are often the kind of people who are teachable because they know that it is in their best interest to learn the shortest, fastest way to get from point A to point B, and they are not fond of wasting time or energy to reinvent the wheel. If we don't teach them the fastest way to succeed, they may go find someone who will teach them and pass us by as if we are standing still.

You could take one of these "runners" and drop them in the middle of a cornfield with a rubber band, a paper clip, and a pencil and they would still figure out a way to make a million dollars! To find a runner with a teachable spirit is truly wonderful. At first we may need to spend a considerable amount of time mentoring them so that they can fly high and straight, but it is not uncommon for these runners to end up not only being able to fly on their own, but also having a whole flock of purpose-driven people flying behind them!

Five separate strategies or one main thing?

Someone may ask, "Do I need to develop five totally different strategies to work with these five different kinds of people?"

Though we certainly will deal differently with people depending on which of these five categories that they fall into, I do not believe that we have to be overly preoccupied with every detail of how we change our approach from one person to another. If we keep "one main thing" right about us, we will exude a charisma that will meet the needs of all five different kinds of people. This "one thing" is to make sure that we keep our commitment level to our vision at 100% at all times.

I mentioned earlier, that *if we keep our minds renewed with the right thoughts on a daily basis we will be able to stay stepped over the line and beyond that point of no return with a 100% commitment to the full manifestation of our vision., This will cause us to keep the right kind of charisma flowing from us at a heart level.* This "charisma" will not only let people know that we are 100% committed to the vision we are sharing with them, but this charisma will also help people to feel better and more confident about themselves when they are in our presence.

Of course to stay on the right side of the line every day will necessitate that we also keep our "Top Five" "Why" reasons identified, and our purpose-based vision vividly clear in our hearts and minds.

If we keep the right kind of charisma flowing from us, all five different kinds of people will get the right message from us as it relates exactly to where they are at that exact moment in their lives.

The "unteachables" will know that they can hang around as long as they don't become a weight that will slow us down, and they will also know from the committed charisma they sense coming from us that it is unacceptable to infect other people with any negatives that they may have as a part of their belief system. The "unteachables" will also know where the door is and that if they really don't want to be involved in positive forward momentum, then sooner or later it will probably make sense for them to leave.

The "rollercoaster people" will get the message from the charisma exuding from us at a heart level that we <u>are not</u> going to take the whole up and down rollercoaster ride with them, because it would drain us of our energy to do so. But they also know that if they ever decide to get off their rollercoaster and get "in the game," we are ready to play ball with them at any given moment, and they will have our 100% commitment and support at that time.

The "incubator people" will receive from our charisma the exact right warm encouraging environment to allow them to continue to incubate, and who knows if one day they might finally hatch out of their egg as a "runner" and surprise everyone!

The "walkers" will get what they need to keep on walking and will know that they are a valuable part of the team.

The "runners" will be inspired by our charisma to keep on running.

All of these five different kinds of people will get exactly what they need from us if we just keep ourselves in the right place: "stepped over the line," 100% committed to the vision, where quitting is not an option for us and keeping our mind renewed with truth-based principles is our top priority on a daily basis. If we keep our thinking right and keep our heart in the right place, the people whom we are "purposed" to mentor will be encouraged and will receive from us the highest quality of leadership and purpose-driven-passion that will inspire them to give it all they've got to go to their next personal higher level, and they will also have a collective vision and desire to help the whole team move forward to achieve unlimited victories.

Chapter

10

Know That It Only Takes a Few People to Accomplish Great Things

A wise leader knows that if you have a few people really committed to the vision, you can move mountains, and if a few people really believe that they will accomplish great things, then "all things are possible to those who truly believe." Even if only two or three people are in total agreement as to the accomplishment of a specific worthwhile destiny-driven cause, their synergy will produce awesome creative power.

An error in judgment that some individuals make is that as they begin sharing their vision, mission, or business opportunity, they do so with the fantasy that within the first ten or twenty people they talk with, they will find the inner circle of people that will help them launch into massive success. If the first ten or twenty people do not get excited and make a 100% commitment, many people get discouraged and quit.

In fact, truly great leaders know that it is always a few select people out of many contacts who are responsible for accomplishing the greatest things in any group or business.

Vilfredo Pareto was an Italian economist who lived from the mid 1800s to the early 1900s. He is credited with the discovery of what has become known as the "Pareto Principle" or the "80/20 Rule."

Studies have been conducted throughout the world by individuals, as well as by organizations and businesses, and though at first his principle was considered to only be a theory, amazingly, on average this "80/20 Rule" has been proven to be very accurate in just about every area of life.

For example:

- 80% of your desired results will be produced by 20% of your efforts, and the other 20% of your desired results will come from the remaining 80% of your efforts

- 80% of the money we make is the result of 20% of our work-related activity. The other 80% of the time and effort we put into what we call "working" usually produces about 20% of our financial income.

Of course the smart thing to do here is to identify exactly which of our activities and efforts make up the 20% that are producing our best results and then do more of whatever that is!!!

- In an organization, a business, or any other group that is working to accomplish a common goal, 80% of the productive work and financial profit will be created by the top 20% of the people. The other 20% of the productive work and financial increase will be produced by the remaining 80% of the people.

- On average, in any business or organization, the top 20% of the people earn 80% of the money, and the other 20% of the money earned is split up amongst the bottom 80% of the people.

The top 20% of the people are producing 80% of the

productivity and profitability, so they reap 80% of the rewards.

What is even more dramatic is that when the top 20% of the people are examined in any organization or business, the "80/20 Rule" still applies!

Example:

Within the top 20% of the people in any business or organization, 80% of the productivity and profitability is created as result of the efforts of the top 20% of the top 20%, which is equal to the top 4% of the total number of people involved!!!!!!!

Four out of a hundred ain't bad!

Let's break this down to its simplest form.

If there are 100 people in an organization, business, or any other group that is working together for a common goal

- 80% of the profitability will be produced by the top 20 people

- 80% of the profitability and productivity within the top 20 people will be produced by the top 20% of the top 20 people which is the top 4 people!!!

The simple truth is that if you or I have 100 people who have joined us in any vision, mission, idea, or business, on average we will have

- 4 people who are runners

- 16 people who are walkers

- 80 people who will fall into the categories of "unteachable," "rollercoaster," or "incubator" people

If you have 4 out of every 100 who are runners and 16 walkers, then you are set up for massive success. Even if your vision or business does not seem to be producing massive results at the very beginning, if you can keep your 4 runners and 16 walkers in place, purpose-driven, and moving forward for enough consecutive days in a row, you are guaranteed, on average and within your sphere of influence, to create enough momentum to become one of the most successful people in your field of endeavor.

Once again the truth sets us free

One of the most powerful things about having the knowledge of this "80/20 Rule" is that we no longer feel as though we are "being rejected" by the bottom 80% of the people whom we work with in any pursuit. We understand that this is just "the way it is." The bottom 80% are just doing what the bottom 80% always do, and that is either produce very little or nothing at all. Of course we are still thankful for the 20% profitability that comes from the efforts of the bottom 80%, but we still are fully aware that the strength and longevity of the organization is being sustained by the runners and walkers.

Just knowing the truth about this will set us free to be encouraged instead of being discouraged.

The average *87% negative self-talk person* would get discouraged and quit if they were working with 100 people and only 4 of them where doing great.

Remember, 87% of the average person's self-talk is negative on a daily basis, and the average person thinks between 40,000 to 50,000 thoughts per day.

If you or I were to go out on the street and conduct a survey, asking some of these "87% negative self-talk people" this question: "If you were the leader of 100 people in business and 4 of them were doing great, 16 of them were doing okay, and 80 of the people were doing little or nothing at all, would you consider yourself a successful leader or would you consider yourself a failure?", what do you think the "average 87% negative self-talk" person's answer would be to that question? That's right; the average person would say, "If only 4 out of a 100 were doing great, I would feel like a failure." The main reason most people would feel like a failure in this situation is because they don't know the truth or "the way it really is."

If we do know the truth, and we have 4 runners working with us, we are excited. Why? Because we know that there are many, many, many multimillion dollar companies that only have 3 or 4 people in top leadership positions who are really driving the company to success. If the top 4% were not present in their place of leadership, then the 16 walkers would probably stop walking, the bottom 80% of the people would disappear, and there would be nothing left.

So **if you have 1 out of 25 or 4 out of 100 who are really on your side and making things happen, then YOU ARE SET UP FOR MASSIVE SUCCESS!!!**

Just keep on building consistent momentum with the 4% and the 16%, and you cannot lose. It is just a matter of time until you break through to see your efforts rewarded in an abundant fashion.

Chapter

11

Discover a Major Key to
Never Finishing Short of Your Goal

Whatever the minimum amount of positive results or business volume it is that you need to make your vision or business successful, keep three times that amount of action via phones calls, meetings and potential business in forward motion. Talk to enough people every day or week that even if two out of three people flat out say no and never want to talk with you again, you could still do great with the one out of three who responded more positively to you. Les Brown taught me a principle through his training and by his daily example. It is the "TTP/TTMP" principle. Talk To People, and if that doesn't work, then Talk To More People. The size of your sphere of influence will, to a great extent, determine the size of your manifested vision with respect to building your dream or your business. The size of your sphere of influence can also be a major factor in the size of your bank account. If you want to become financially free, but you are not willing to drive or fly a few hours to meet some new people, then you probably will not reach your highest potential level. In most any business, vision, or mission, there is a local, a regional, a national, and an international potential sphere of influence and opportunity for expansion and growth.

The more mobile we are willing to be, the greater pool

of possibilities there will be for us to maximize.

With the advantage of the Internet and the widespread use of computers has come the opportunity for just about anyone to expand worldwide.

Years ago I did most of my traveling within the United States, but in recent years, since I have developed my Web site, I receive invitations to speak at conferences, receive emails, and orders for my books, tapes, and CDs from just about every country on earth. I am also grateful to the many great leaders who have distributed my books and audio programs within their organizations in over fifty countries around the world.

We are truly living in an amazing time in history. It still boggles my mind that I can sit down at my computer, type out an email message, click Send, and a few seconds later that email message pops up on a computer screen in Australia! The World Wide Web is an amazing tool that just about anyone can use to turbo charge their vision or business.

However, I must say that with all of the advantages the Internet provides, we must be careful to not rely too much on the convenience of emailing people instead of calling them on the phone. No matter how useful the tools of email and a Web site may be, they will never replace the need for one-on-one contact with people. Making the phone calls, meeting with people, mentoring others, and being mentored by a leader to whom we have submitted ourselves are all irreplaceable aspects of building a strong vision. No matter how "high tech" we get, those more non-personal methods will never replace what people feel when they hear our voice or shake our hand. The Internet, email, and computers should be used only as secondary tools. Our primary tool for building rapport and relationships will always be our personal "voice to voice" or "face to face" contact.

As we keep our relationships with the key people in our lives our top priority, we can then use the Internet effectively as a secondary tool to give us access to the whole world like nothing else can. The ability to expand our vision or business worldwide is now more obtainable than ever before.

With this ability to expand your vision to a wider scope than was probable in the past comes the necessity for you to get into your car or get on a plane and travel longer distances than most people were used to traveling years ago.

In addition to speaking at many conferences, events, and publicly promoted exclusive workshops throughout the United States, during the next twelve months I have also been invited to speak in seven other countries which will require traveling a distance of five to ten thousand miles per speaking engagement.

If you would have told me twenty years ago that I would be traveling long-distance like this on a regular basis, I might not have believed you. At first glance, one can view this kind of traveling as being a very glamorous lifestyle, but in reality it is hard work. Yet all of the car trips, airplane travel, hotel stays, packing, and unpacking are well worth the effort. The rewards gained by being willing to get out of our comfort zone in order to be highly mobile always far outweigh the effort invested in doing so.

One of the sideline benefits that expanding beyond your city, your region, your country, and finally having a vision to expand worldwide is the advantage of meeting people who can help you gain wisdom, secrets, and insights that may not be readily available to you in your hometown.

One of the perks that comes along with racking up a lot of frequent flyer miles each year is that the airlines will upgrade you to first class seating on just about every flight that you take. An advantage of sitting in first class is that you get to meet some very interesting and very successful people. I have received a wealth of knowledge and inspiration while talking with some of these folks up in the front of the plane! On a flight from Las Vegas to Detroit, the National Sales Manager for one of the top internationally known vacuum cleaner companies told me that the sales reps in his company always, without exception, make a sale to one out of every three people to whom they demonstrate his company's $3000-$4000 product, and his sales people make a 50% commission. He told me that his product is so great that "even the people who do not do a good presentation" often still sell to one out of three people. I thought, "Wow, even if they did three presentations a day and sold only one product per day, that is still an income of $1500-$2000 per day, and that's pretty good money". I asked the sales manager, "With sales numbers like one out of three, your people must make a lot of money?" He said. "Yes, some of my reps make thousands of dollars a day, but most of them only make one or two sales per month!!!! "Why?" I asked. He said "Because, to get three people to allow one of my sales representatives to share his or her presentation with them, she or he will on average, have to make sixty trips to sixty houses before finding one person who is willing to let that sales representative into the house and take the time to watch the demonstration and listen to the sales pitch."!!!!

There is no shortcut for getting around the need to take massive action and expand your sphere of influence.

At times people may say to someone who has achieved great things or has been a blessing to many people, "It must be wonderful to receive all the thanks, the praise, and the positive feedback that you receive from being a blessing to thousands of people." The person's response to this flattery could very well be something like this: "Yes, I must admit it does feel good, and it is also very humbling. But I also know the price I had to pay before I was given the opportunity to reach large numbers of people with a message of hope and freedom."

I remember years ago when it was not uncommon for me to leave two hundred phone messages or voice mails with secretaries or prospects, and then maybe have only five or ten people return my calls. I worked for years to overcome feelings of rejection while contacting new people who didn't know me, and at times it felt as if they considered my phone calls an intrusion or an inconvenience. I learned that if you want people to care about who you are and what you do, you will have to earn their respect. Before that respect is earned, some people may treat us as though they really don't care about us or about the benefits we believe we can provide to them! And there are some people who are just downright rude, negative, and abrasive. To find the wonderful, precious group of leaders that I now have the privilege of working with worldwide, I had to pay an upfront price before being able to enjoy all of my present blessings. I have found that after we have "paid the initial price" to get our personal vision off the ground and flying, it is best not to be overly impressed by the things we have accomplished, but rather we should continually raise the bar and be more impressed with the amazing potential that still lies ahead.

I am thankful, humbled, and encouraged when people validate my purpose and worth, but I also remember the many times when I wanted to quit and give up. And even though I realize that my effort and my persistence contributed to my life being so blessed, I also know that it is still only by the grace of God that I have been allowed to come this far.

I am acutely aware of the fact that I am indebted to the many great leaders with whom I am blessed to work, as well as to all of the leaders who continually promote my work, my teaching materials, and invite me to speak to their groups and organizations. It is true that at first, it will be you who will create the momentum to get your vision-plane off the ground, but to continue to fly; you will need other leaders to fly in formation with you. Some of the leaders will fly ahead of you, some will fly beside you on the left or on the right, and some of the leaders you work with will fly behind you, as you provide mentorship to help them lead others. As you continually flow in the right kind of charisma, you will attract more and more great leaders unto yourself. The collective agreement, vision, wisdom, unity (and many additional things you will receive and share with other leaders) will cause you and them to fly to greater heights than any of you could achieve alone.

I awoke at 3:00 AM one morning with my mind and heart filled with inspiring thoughts that I wanted to capture. I knew that if I allowed myself to go back to sleep I would loose most of these thoughts forever. So, I got out of bed, walked into my office, picked up a tape recorder, and spoke some words into the microphone. Then I went back to bed and fell asleep again. The next day I gave the tape to my wife, Julie, and I asked her if she would please type out the words that I had recorded onto that tape. Julie said, "Sure, I would be happy to type it out for you." The following few paragraphs contain the words that were on that tape recording. Some of the grammar and punctuation in these next few paragraphs may be a little choppy, but I have left it that way on purpose so that you get the raw form in which these thoughts were born.

"It's not the ones with a silver spoon in their mouths when they were born. It's not the ones who seem to have all the cards stacked in their favor. It's the persistent one that wins out. It's the one who makes the most phone calls and can keep the right charisma flowing from their heart. It's not the one who starts out with all the best contacts and connections. It's not the one who's voted most likely to succeed. Many who seem like they will, won't and many who seem like they won't, will. It does not depend on having the best oratory and linguistics. Many times it is the one who is just resilient enough to keep inching forward, to fail and succeed, and succeed and fail, and fail and succeed again. Until finally they break through and find those significant people who are going to be the ones who will join them in leadership and build something tremendous. It's not necessarily the one that popular opinion would elect to be the great leader. It's the one that knows that they know that they know... The one who will pay the price to keep the right thoughts - to live in the truth and flow in that indescribable charisma that causes others to have confidence in them. It is the one that lives every day planting the right "thought-seeds" in their heart and mind. The one whose desire for something better…gives birth to a discipline of meditating on the truth day and night…night and day and day and night. That is the person who ends up exuding the kind of charisma that attracts the right people into their sphere of influence. And by attracting the right people unto themselves they build a group of leaders who they can work with and be proud of. A group of leaders that are committed to them and they are committed to those… They join together in destiny to create freedom for all who would have the vision to stand with them.

No, it is not the one that seems to have all the natural advantage. It is not guaranteed to the one who says "I have the right family heritage". It is the one who says "It is worth it for me to pay the price and do whatever is necessary to birth my dream into reality". It is the one who makes freedom their top priority. It's the one who says "God Almighty has given me the right, yes, and even the birthright to be free in every area of my life – spiritually, mentally, emotionally, in my relationships and, yes free financially". The one who is convicted in their very heart of hearts and their very soul of souls...with total submission to the mission. Their words reveal their abundant hearts, as they speak their faith... "I know freedom is what I was born for and I am all about finding my inner circle of leaders who see the vision... who know that this is the main thing – that this is the preeminent thing... that our families will not be free until somebody holds up the torch – that my life will not be free as an example to others until I first pay the price to know that I know, that I know, that I know... This is not just a notion, but I stand on the truth that has been laid down long before I was born. Knowing the truth, I am set free. All those that I can help to come to the place where they are in a knowing of the truth will be free as well. God has created us to be free in every area of our lives. This freedom is not just reserved for spiritual freedom, though that is the highest and best. It is not just reserved for freedom in relationships, though that is second to the top. But it is also reserved for financial freedom. When I am financially free, it sets me at liberty to not have to worry about money and to put my energy and my efforts into that which is most meaningful, because I am no longer preoccupied with lack thoughts.

No, it's not being born into the right family... that is not the main key. It's not whether everything goes properly, and everything flows smoothly. In fact, challenges will come, storms will arise, but I know that I know, that I know why I was born – the purpose for which I was placed here was to lead many to freedom. And as I keep my commitment to that purpose – that, in itself, will set me on a course that will cause me to see every man and every woman as someone who I was born to plant a seed of freedom in. If it begins to grow in them, then I will see a sprout and I will know that that is a person who I am supposed to work with in a way of gentleness and humility until finally that sprout becomes a tender young tree and that tree becomes a mighty oak and that mighty oak then towers up into the heavens as a testimony and as a flag flying high for all to witness. All can look and see that they can be free as well.

No, it's not where you're born. It's not where you're placed at the beginning of your life. It's not how much money you have to get started. It's not how many contacts you have to work with initially. It is whether you are driven by a passion-powered-purpose. It is whether you will continue on until you find the gold that is hidden. It is whether you will talk with enough people until you find the few that you were meant to be with all along. It is if you are willing to talk to "the many" to find "the few". They are hidden amongst the stony ground of life. Dig out as you would mine for gold, those precious ones who will stand with you for the cause of freedom — who will stand with you and say "I will pay the price, I was born to be free".

Let us go forth on a mission. Let us go forth with destiny beating in our breasts. Keep sorting through people to find those who are ready to hear. Those who hear the sound of freedom will hear the hearkening of your voice and they will say "Yes, I join together with you, I count the cost, and I determine that I will pay the price. No determination, no persistence is too much of a price to pay. Freedom is so valuable that I am willing to be one of those freedom fighters who will join with you and we will stand shoulder to shoulder and go through whatever is necessary to be persons who can say, "I have realized freedom and look at all of these that I have been able to be a blessing to and they are now living on a level of freedom themselves."

Yes, it is the one who resolves that their calling, their purpose, their mission — is to fulfill the freedom that God Almighty has placed in the heart of every woman and every man and has made available to every human being. The freedom that we find is to a great extent, as a result of the leader who first spoke the word to us… and then they laid out the plan that made freedom possible and finally, as we develop a strong team of leaders…freedom becomes inevitable! The plan and the way to freedom has been proven by those who have gone before us and worn a path that we may follow. Anything less than total freedom is less than what we were created to live. Spiritual, mental, emotional, relationship, and yes, financial freedom is our birthright. Freedom is much more than just a good idea. Freedom is God's idea.

It is undeniable that one of the most fortifying forces in equipping us to be resilient enough to overcome all forms of rejection is the power that is produced when we join together in unity with like-minded people for the accomplishment of a worthwhile cause.

Chapter

12

Use Rejection to Help Drive You to Your Next Higher Level

Most of the rejection that we face is quite mild in comparison to the threat a soldier faces on the battlefield while defending the freedom of his or her country or the threat that firefighters face when they rush into a burning building to save lives. Most of the rejection we face has no element of physical threat, but it does have the potential to injure our ego, our self image, and our sense of worthiness. If we let it affect us, the fear of rejection will stunt our growth and may even kill our dreams.

By overcoming the fear of rejection, we not only remove rejection's ability to harm us, but we also gain the courage to step over the line into new territory and create new breakthroughs in our lives.

There is a true story I heard years ago which illustrates how freedom from fear causes rejection to lose its power to hold us back from going to our next higher level.

This story is about a man who "stepped over a line and went beyond the point of no return" to pursue his dream, his vision, his purpose, and his mission in life. When he made a one hundred percent commitment to his mission, the fear of rejection disappeared, and his dream was manifested.

This man was a missionary who felt very strongly that he was purposed to help a tribe of head-hunters receive medical aid to cure a disease epidemic that was running rampant amongst the tribe members and threatening their very existence. He tried to approach this tribe for several months, but each time he got near, he was scared off for fear of losing his life.

This tribe was known to be fierce cannibals. They were not only cannibalistic but were also known to shrink the heads of those they had killed and to keep the shrunken heads as trophies.

One night this missionary had a dream, and in the dream an angel spoke to him and asked, "Do you want to live your life fearing death, or is your purpose important enough to you that you would be willing to die in the pursuit of your destiny?" He answered the angel, "I would rather die than live the rest of my life knowing I did not complete the mission that I was born to fulfill".

The next morning the missionary woke up, and the fear of losing his life was gone. He believed with all his heart that he was going to see a breakthrough take place as he moved forward with no fear but only love in his heart for these tribal members.

The next day he approached the tribe without fear and gave them a gift of food and clothing. With a new purpose-driven charisma he made many short visits to the tribe, each time bringing them different gifts. Though at first the people would not let him make any physical contact with them, over time the tribe's people came to trust him to the point that they actually allowed him to put a hypodermic needle into their arms to inject medicines and vaccines that stopped the spread of the diseases that had been threatening the tribe's existence. The missionary also supplied the tribe with spiritual support and agricultural assistance, and finally he was celebrated by the tribe as a great hero!

After his work with the tribe had became a well-known success among other missionaries, one of his colleagues asked, "What was the change that occurred to you after you had that dream, and how did you get the courage that enabled you to achieve such great success?" His response was, **"I literally lost the fear of death, and after I was no longer afraid to die, what else could that tribe threaten me with?"**

Most of us will not have to face the risk of being physically killed in the pursuit of our dreams, but let me once again ask this question, "What difference would it make in your ability to build a vision, mission, or business if you lost just one thing, that thing called "the fear of people"? It would make a huge difference.

The following few paragraphs came to me as I once again awoke very early one morning. . This time it was 4:07 AM. I got out of bed, went to my office, picked up my hand-held tape recorder with a built-in microphone, and I began to speak the thoughts that filled my mind and heart. Later that morning, as I did with the transcript of the earlier recording, I asked my wife, Julie, to type out the words from this second recording. These are the words that were on that tape:

A Friend Called Rejection

I think it's a good idea to have a dialogue with rejection and say, "Hi, Rejection. I've become fairly acquainted with you throughout my life and I realize that you're probably going to be there just about every step of the way...as I pursue my goals, my dreams, my vision, and my purpose, so therefore, I've decided to not allow you to be my adversary.

I've decided to become your friend and as your friend, I want to tell you the truth.

The truth is that you are not going to stop me and the truth is, that no matter what you say or do or try to put upon me, I am not going to give in to (lend credence to) your opinions or observations about me or my dream.

I'm not going to buy into it.

So, feel free to use people.

Feel free to use circumstances.

Feel free to use money shortages.

Feel free to use whatever techniques you might feel that you want to use, but know this: it doesn't matter what techniques, methods or people you use, you're not going to get to me. In fact, I am going to use you as a tool that is going to strengthen me.

Rejection, in the same way that an eagle cups it's wings when the storm is coming and uses the power of the oncoming storm to drive it higher, I am going to use the turbulence that you create in my life to drive me higher and higher and higher and higher...

Rejection, the more that you turn up the heat, the more you're going to be helping me to go higher in life.

So, friend, I am not going to get stressed out when you're around. I'm not going to get perplexed when you're present. I am literally going to rest in the fact that if I keep my mind and my heart on truth...then God will keep my mind and heart in perfect peace.

Rejection, I know that you will always be there, but you know what, instead of you being my hinderer, I have decided to use you as my helper and I appreciate all the help you're going to give me.

There are times that you're going to get me so ticked-off and sick 'n tired of being sick and tired that that's going to be the inspiration and motivation that's going to push me forward.

You're going to get me out of my comfort zones, but let this be clear: You are never going to convince me that I'm on the wrong path. You're never going to convince me that my dream cannot become a manifested reality. You're never going to convince me that the lies that negative people are saying about me are true.

All you're going to do is be an aid and help in putting a fire underneath me that is going to cause me to run after my dream with more passion and more purpose than ever before.

Thank you, for giving me another reason to go forward full speed ahead, because I know, Rejection, that you are a liar. You'll always lie. That's all you ever do. That's the only tool that you've got to use, is lying.

The way that I'll know that you're lying will always be very easy to distinguish. I'll know you're lying whenever your lips are moving.

Every time I hear your voice, that'll just give me more of a hunger to dig down and find the truth that will shut you up...that will cause you to be totally impotent and powerless as I continue in a hot pursuit for my purpose and my next higher level.

Okay, Rejection, give it the best shot you've got, but know that I'm going to turn all of the obstacles that you put in front of me into opportunities. I'm going to turn all of the troubles that you place before me into triumphs and I'm going to use every mountain you create as a means for my greater momentum."

Yes, overcoming rejection will make you rich. Rich in the love of family and friends, rich mentally, rich emotionally, rich spiritually, with the peace of knowing that God did not create you to be a second-class citizen of this world. Rich in knowing that you were born to live your best life now...Rich in purpose and fulfillment, rich in a lifestyle that will allow you and your family to enjoy all the wonderful things and travel to all the wonderful places on God's good earth, and yes, also rich in financial wealth. The greatest among you will be the one who learns how to be the best servant. As you give, so you shall receive. If you try to bless and help people, and some of them reject you, there is no need to let it affect you in any way, shape, or form. What others think or say about you does not change the truth of who you really are on the inside. Whether they accept you or reject the gift of your giving spirit does not change the fact that you were created to live a life of total freedom. It is humbling to know that we did not create the idea that we are supposed to be abundantly free in every area of our life. We are simply fulfilling our destiny. You were born to be the head and not the tail, above and not beneath. All forms of rejection are temporary, but your purpose is permanent. Rich is the person who still loves and believes in people, even when there is the possibility of being rejected. Rich is the person who believes in others until some of those other people begin to believe in themselves.

You were born to be on a winning team. You were born to find your team of leaders with which to build a vision and a life of freedom.

When the dust settles, it should not be the ones who rejected you who determine how high you will fly. It is the precious people that you have found with hearts that beat with the same rhythm as yours. **IT'S ALL ABOUT FREEDOM. When you know the truth, the truth always sets you free. When you are free from the misguided opinions of other people and the misguided thoughts that try to plant their seeds in your mind...rejection can't touch you, and it will never stop you from moving forward...GO FORTH AND CREATE THE FREEDOM THAT IS YOUR BIRTHRIGHT.**

About the Author

Larry DiAngi is living proof that the principles he shares will work if you "work them". He delivers keynote speeches and conducts seminars for both business and public audiences around the world. Larry is the author of the book, *The Resilient Power of Purpose*, (formerly titled: *How To Be Purpose Driven*) which is presently in its eleventh printing and has been sold worldwide in over 50 different countries. Larry is also author of the book *The Magic Is In The Extra Mile*, which is now in its seventh printing,

During his early years it seemed unlikely that he would do anything significant in life. Then, at age 17 he began a relentless study of individuals who had found purpose, meaning and success in their own lives. This pursuit developed into a passion to share what he was learning with others.

His experiences in life and constant quest for principles that produce real results, prepared him to share these principles with people from all walks of life. From playing drums in rock bands, to working on an assembly line, to selling fire extinguishers door to door to businesses, spending time in the ministry, counseling at a home for juvenile delinquents, being a sales director for a local magazine, then becoming president of a corporation. For years he also hosted a weekly television show on an ABC affiliate while also hosting a daily radio program. Larry moved on to speak to audiences nationally and internationally as he has continued to do for the past eighteen years. He has become a sought after resource for personal and professional development.

Larry's mission is to give people principles that will help them to discover and live from the inspiration of their purpose, to create breakthroughs, and go on to make their dreams a reality.

Smell of popcorn + attraction
Smell of rotten food + away.

OTHER BOOK AND CD SELECTIONS
BY LARRY DiANGI

Book: "The Resilient Power Of Purpose" (Formerly titled "How To Be Purpose Driven") (Over 150,000 Sold)

Book: "The Magic Is In The Extra Mile" (Over 120,000 Sold)

CD Programs:

"OWN YOUR DREAM" The Resilient Power Of Purpose
(When you renew your thoughts you will recreate your life.)
    6 CD series with study manual (Full length live recordings from two live seminars, plus six studio personal coaching sessions)

"PURSUING YOUR PURPOSE WITH A PASSION"
    4 CD Series

"EIGHT DYNAMIC POWER STEPS TO ACHIEVING YOUR GOALS"
    4 CD Series

"BREAKTHROUGH LEADERSHIP" (A quantum leap to higher levels of life, business and wealth.)
    12 CD Series

THESE PRODUCTS ARE AVAILABLE FOR ORDERING ONLINE AT:

www.larrydiangi.com

**For information about booking
Larry DiAngi to present a speech
or workshop at your next event,
please call 1-800-690-1372**